Sandy

8-17-19

FROM LOCKDOWN TO FREEDOM

Genesis 50:20

REV. 22:20

IL 12:11

MAY THIS BOOK BE
A BIG ENCOURAGEMENT
TO YOU & MANY OTHERS

Ron Zaucha

RON ZAUCHA
WITH NOLA KATHERINE

Ron Zaucha
P O Box 3712
Laguna Hills, CA 92654
949-599-4212 Fax 949-860-7009

ISBN (Print Edition): 978-1-54394-743-4

ISBN (eBook Edition): 978-1-54394-744-1

I dedicate *From Lockdown to Freedom* to…

God Almighty for my salvation through Jesus Christ.

The families and individuals I have hurt directly and indirectly. I pray they will forgive me for the pain and sorrow I have caused them.

My precious mother, for all the heartbreaking things I put her through. My mom was the best mother a man could hope to have. In spite of her shortcomings, which we all have, she sacrificed her life for her kids. And for that, I will be eternally grateful. I cannot thank her enough for her unconditional love, care, and support and for sticking with me and never giving up on me. I would never have made it without her. She was my rock.

The friends I left behind the walls. I pray daily for them, asking God to put a hedge of protection around them as I trust Jesus, who is in the business of changing lives…even behind prison walls.

My ex-wife, Rhonda, who never gave up on me and gave her all to stand by me before our marriage and the many years we dated after our sep-aration. She loved me enough to endure much heartache and sorrow I caused her waiting for me to change. Eventually, I did change, but it was too late to save our relationship. For this, I will be forever broken hearted to not have this special lady in my life. Choices have consequences, and I have no one to blame but myself.

And last but not least, to the seven men who met with me weekly for seven years as they poured the foundations of prayer into my life. They became my prayer partners and sustained me throughout one of the most challenging periods of my life. Thank you, Mark Reed, Joseph Hughes, Norm Blackmer, Jeff Birch, Eve Lundgren, Johnny Carrillo, and Eddie Howard.

In Memory of Wally Nelson

I honor the memory of Wally Nelson who saw something in me that I could not see in myself. Without his godly love and wisdom, I would not be in prison ministry today. I will be forever grateful to God for allowing me to be mentored and taught by this godly man who eventually became my trusted friend. Wally loved Jesus and his family, and hundreds of men like me who did not deserve the mercy and grace of God we received because of his prison ministry.

"When I began serving as the Protestant Chaplain at California Institution for Women (CIW) State Prison in 1998, Pastor Ron was already serving as a Religious Volunteer.

"Therefore I salute him for over 20 years of faithful service to CIW. I came to know him as a very straight-forward person. He would go into the chapel fully prepared and ready to preach with boldness the genuine gospel of Jesus Christ. Once I got to know him and his past life as a prison inmate, I understood his seriousness in helping other prison inmates to receive their salvation. God took a radical sinner from behind the prison walls and turned him into a humble saint serving those behind prison walls and beyond. I am sure his book, *From Lockdown to Freedom,* will be an eye-opener to all who read it, especially those behind prison walls. Congratulations, Pastor Ron for a job well done."

Rev. Lois M. Woodard, Protestant Chaplain (CIW) and Pastor, New Allen Chapel AME Church, Delano, California.

"If you want evidence of a life dramatically changed by the grace of God through Jesus Christ, then meet Ron Zaucha. Ron's miraculous encounter with Jesus, when he was a prison inmate, led him into prison ministry. Consequently, Ron discovered that thousands of people serving time all across the country were just like he was…lost in sin, crime, hate, and anger. They felt alone and forgotten by the rest of the world. Ron's desire to reach out and let other lost souls know that God cares about them, no matter what they have done, led him into ministry in 1993 and to be the founder of Lighthouse Educational Ministries Inc. in 1996. His ministry has influenced over 30,000 people to make a life-changing decision for Jesus Christ. *From Lockdown to Freedom* is an essential read for those who have lost their way in life. As Jesus Christ miraculously changed the life of Ron Zaucha, He will do the same for you."

Pastor Ron Keller is retired Senior Pastor at Christ's Church of the Valley, San Dimas, California. He is currently, teacher of the Adult Bible Class, Mariners Church, Irvine, California, and teaches at HaDavar Messianic Ministries, Community Church of Irvine, Irvine, California.

"Ron, an American Californian boy, who lived the lifestyle of a hustler and drug dealer to the rich and famous, didn't trust anyone except his two best friends (Smith & Wesson), Ron carried his guns alongside his flamboyant lifestyle of being rich. Ron started to see what the fast lane had to offer, failing to realize there's a price that comes with it that neither drugs, money, nor sex could bring. Instead, Ron would find himself sitting in a prison cell until he had a close encounter with the Lord himself. Upon his release, at an Easter Sunday service, he discovered God had a plan for his life. Today, Ron travels and shares his life experiences and how a real transformation takes place in one's life when one surrenders their all to Jesus Christ! It's an honor and privilege to have ministered alongside Ron and see a faithful servant at work carrying with him the two most important things in his life, the Word of God and Jesus Christ."

Chaplain Mark Maciel, D.T.S., holds two Masters, one in Counseling and the other in Theology as well as a Doctorate in Theology. He served as Chaplain for L.A. County Sheriff's Department for 20 years, He is a motivational speaker, an author, and teaches training and evangelizing in prisons all over the US. He travels with the Bill Glass Ministry Team and works with churches to organize prison ministries. He is Assistant Pastor at Calvary Chapel Downey and serves in various positions in a wide range of ministries. He is currently Executive Director of Prison Ministry of America.

"I have known Ron Zaucha for many years. Ron had submitted an application to come into the prison to share the Gospel with those who were still incarcerated. Ron's book, *From Lockdown to Freedom*, is an account of how God has given Ron purpose and direction in his life. I am confident that when you read this book, it will be a blessing to you and inspire you to be all you can be for the Lord Jesus Christ."

Pastor Albert Davis Sr., Jericho Christian Fellowship

"I know Ron's story to be as real as they come. His testimony will give you hope where hope may have been lost. Ron's story of how Jesus redeemed his life will encourage you to bring others to faith in Jesus Christ. Get this book into the hands of someone you love."

Pastor Mike Mailo, Senior Pastor Mission Viejo Christian Church, Mission Viejo, California.

"It has been an honor and a privilege to spend time with Ron, to get to know him and to co-author his incredible, redemptive story. As we spent long hours struggling to pull his story together, we shed a few tears along the way, stepped on each other's toes, and found reasons to laugh at things that were really not funny. Although our journeys are very different, I realized right away that we *get* each other. He has become more than a friend; he has become my brother-in-Christ. Ron is a giant of a man whose very presence was once terrifying to those around him. However, he has become a gentle giant among men. His big voice, contagious laughter, caring heart, and love for Jesus cause men and women in the penal system to listen to his story and believe they too can find renewed hope for their lives. Ron has exceptional wisdom that he can only share because he has lived in the deep darkness of the soul and understands its power. In *From Lockdown to Freedom*, Ron humbles himself and tells it like it is! His story is raw, honest, and heartbreaking, but will bring healing, freedom, and joy to your heart as you turn the last page and close the book. Thank you, Ron, for touching my life and giving me the opportunity to spread my wings a little wider."

Nola Katherine, author, I Can Begin Again, Inside the Mind of an Adult Who was Abused as a Child, co-author, ghostwriter, speaker.

"I've been a Christian since the age of 11 years old, and I've heard many stories of people who have been changed by the power of God. However, when I heard Ron's story, I was truly overcome and taken back by the depth of his pain and sorry for the life that he led and the number of people he negatively affected. A serious bad-boy had become a real man of God. I now have the privilege to serve with Ron at the Chino Women's Prison; where I can witness his love for the Lord and desire to serve others. As a Licensed Marriage & Family Therapist, with an understanding of the severe effects of drugs and alcohol, I am amazed at Ron's ability to quote Scripture and preach the gospel to the inmates. This is indeed a story of redemption!"

Kathy A. Stone, Licensed Marriage & Family Therapist

"In the often hard-boiled, 'take no prisoners' world of law I operate in, Ron Zaucha is a breath of fresh air: scrupulously honest, always empathic and kind, and never willing to compromise his religion or ethics for the expedient. This book is no exception."

Robert Ouriel, Attorney

"As friends at Central Baptist Church of Pomona, I had the privilege of knowing Ron Zaucha's mother before I knew him. I became acquainted with Ron in April on a Sunday morning when he came forward saying that he wanted to accept the Lord Jesus Christ as his personal Savior. He also said that he was out of jail on bail because his grandmother put up the bond, but that he would have to go back to jail and serve his sentence. I kept in touch with him through his mother. I asked him to get in touch with me when he got out of jail, which he did. I gave him a job in my warehouse. We have continued to be consistent friends throughout all the many years. I know he has a burning desire to win souls for the Lord through prison ministry. I went with him on visitation in the local prisons and saw why he has a strong desire to win souls to Christ. I love him and want God's continued blessing upon his ministry, as well as his own personal life."

Dallas M Beaird, an independent contractor who built schools and churches for twenty years.

ACKNOWLEDGMENT

I want to thank my co-author, Nola Katherine with all my heart. God put her in my life at a time when I thought my book would never come together for publication. I gave her my rough draft, and she turned it into a compelling story. She sifted through hundreds of notes and spent many long hours listening to me and putting the information together. Her gift of organization and her gift with words gave me hope that someday this work would be completed. She is a loving, giving person, and she has become more than a friend, she has become my sister-in-Christ. Thank you, Nola Katherine, for giving me more than two years of your life. I pray God will return it a hundredfold.

CONTENTS

FOREWORD

I am honored and blessed to write the foreword to *From Lockdown to Freedom* by Ron Zaucha, my dear friend, and Brother in Christ. I instantly bonded with Ron at a function for Pastor Mark Maciel many years ago. The real cement was our relationship with Jesus Christ and our prison ministry. Brother Ron had seen several movies that I did, so we talked and shared our testimonies. This was where our 20-year plus friendship started, and we have ministered together all these years.

I have observed how God made Ron into a new creation (2 Corinthians 5:17). His compelling book outlines the many choices that put him in prison. Yes, he was the man who dealt drugs to celebrities and to many others all over the country. He had the women, drugs, and money. He carried two guns on him most of the time, but as always those in that lifestyle have a deep void...an emptiness. Only Jesus could fill that ocean of nothingness. That was when Ron cried out to God, "If you are real, show me..." He was arrested the next day, and God showed him in prison. That is where God really got his attention. Brokenness will do that. All those years of pride, ego, and rebellion brought him to his knees. Now God is able to do amazing things in Ron's life, and I have personally witnessed his transformation first hand.

There was a time when Ron was ready to get out of ministry because of some conflicts he had with a couple of pastors at a church he attended. I drove a long way to participate in that meeting. They wanted me to go against Ron and his prison ministry, which I refused to do. He is my friend and Brother in Christ. We met at a coffee shop to discuss his future in ministry. He was depressed, heartbroken, felt rejected and abandoned. I basically said, "Shape up and start your own ministry." Ron did, and the rest is history.

You will be blessed by this book. I am proud of Ron and praise God for his ministry and our friendship.

Mel Novak is a dedicated Soldier-for-Christ, an actor and an ordained minister called by God to share Jesus to the homeless on skid row and in prisons.

INTRODUCTION

I can remember it as though it happened yesterday. Thud! Thud! Thud! In drumbeat rhythm was the sound of baseball bats hitting heads, backs, arms, and legs. We swung our bats at the four boys, who appeared to be our own ages. I struck with all the anger and raging fury of one who had no conscience, no heart, and no soul. I heard the cruel sound in my ears...the sound of bones cracking. I saw the blood...dripping, splattering in every direction. I smelled their fear as it hung thick in the night air. But, I could not smell my own fear. I was numb.

It is hard to go back and dig up my past. It is something I am not proud of. Yet, my past defines who I was for many years. I was bound in a prison of unimaginable sin...a life of crime, hatred and immoral acts. I lived in lockdown for most of my life...held captive by family dysfunction, peer pressure, cultural norms, faulty thinking, ignorance, and deception. Eventually, sin's foundation crumbled and because of the hope and prayers of my mother, grandmother, and ex-wife, my life was changed. I was set free from the chains that bound me.

I tell my story to give hope to others who are traveling down the road of destruction I once traveled. I want others to understand that *lockdown* is more than being an inmate in prison. Depression, anger, shame, hate, unforgiveness, as well as child abuse and physical and emotional abuse will keep them mentally and emotionally confined to prisons without bars. I desire that those who feel their lives are in *lockdown* understand they do not have to remain stuck in a prison with or without bars.

It is my prayer those who read my story will find the real freedom and peace I have found. More importantly, it is my hope they will discover the *object* of my newfound freedom, Jesus Christ. My name is Ron Zaucha, and I invite you into my wild and crazy world through the telling of my story which begins and ends in the state of California. This is the story of my life, *From Lockdown to Freedom.*

Please note that some persons, places or things mentioned in *From Lockdown to Freedom* have been changed out of respect, and others have been changed for protection.

CHAPTER 1

MOB MENTALITY

Understanding My Family Roots

"So what does the Chicago Mob have to do with me anyway?" My Aunt Ellen's eyes locked with mine. I felt her steadfast gaze as I tried to process what she was saying to me. "Ron, don't you get it? We come from a family that was involved in the Chicago Mob?" I knew just enough about the mob to know it was dangerous and something I had no interest in being a part of. I had heard my dad tell some really crazy stories, but as a kid, they were just stories. I had not connected any of them to our family in Chicago and definitely not to my family in California. I was taken aback to learn my grandfather, on my dad's side of the family, had ties to the Polish Mafia in Chicago and how our family's connection to it affected my dad in many negative ways.

Since I was just a young boy, my aunt had watched the rage I had toward my father slowly building. She rightly discerned there was constant turmoil churning within me that had the potential for turning into something deadly. She realized I needed answers to questions I didn't even know to ask, and that I needed to understand why my father had treated me as though I had no feelings...that I did not matter.

But I was no longer a little boy, and Aunt Ellen feared the path my own life was taking. She hoped she could help me avoid the pitfalls of my father. However, it would be many years before I truly understood that many of the perils awaiting me were the results of my family roots.

Since I do not have actual records, I can only speculate what my grandfather's timeline might look like based on the information given to me. He would have been born sometime around the turn of the 20th century when Poland, as a country, did not exist. Old Poland was absorbed into Prussia, Russia, and Austria in the late 1790s but was reconstituted as a republic in 1918 after WWI. Following the war, political turmoil resulted in economic and structural changes in central Europe. These changes created an instability that probably prompted my grandparents to sail to America with the hope of a better life. Polish migration to the United States actually began in the 1850s. Hence a vibrant Polish community had already been established when they arrived in Chicago by train, perhaps around 1920.

Apparently, like many before him, life in America was not as Grandfather Zaucha had hoped for. Chicago was just as bad or worse than Poland but in very different ways. However, prohibition laws established by the US federal government in 1920 created a way for my dad's father to provide for his family. In fact, many small-time Polish-American criminal gangs developed because downtrodden immigrants like my grandfather discovered they could make money through bootlegging, the illegal sale of alcohol.

I was shocked to realize how much Aunt Ellen knew about mob activity. Frightening images raced through my mind as I listened to her reveal information previously held in secrecy. It did not take long for me to see the big picture she was painting for me.

Although lucrative, bootlegging was a brutal and violent business. Mobsters had power and took unfair advantage of law-abiding business owners because the mobster mostly wanted to use legitimate businesses as a front for their illegal activity. These gangsters used sawed-off shotguns, machine guns, baseball bats, or threats to intimidate them to their way of thinking. Anyone who was confronted by a criminal honing in on their business knew they must give in for fear of being executed or severely beaten. The scare tactics worked.

In the 1930s, gangsters were secretly sent to labor unions in the city of Chicago to gain power over illegal bootlegging, gambling and prostitution. To make matters worse, the gangs began to battle against each other for control. For a time, the Windy City became an upside-down universe. To get immunity, when criminals were busted by the Feds, they would offer bribes to police and politicians in the districts where these gangsters operated. It became difficult to tell who the legal or illegal business partner was. For instance, the businessman was a politician, the politician was a gangster, and the gangster was a businessman. It became difficult to stop or even to prosecute these criminals. Any opposition, including witnesses who were called to testify against mob activities or enraged union members, was immediately killed by the gangsters. It was an awful time in our American history but, according to my aunt, it was also a terrible time for my Polish-Immigrant family who experienced it firsthand.

I did not grasp just how much these conditions impacted my dad until my mother filled in the missing pieces. "Your grandfather was killed when your dad was a teenager, in all probability because of his involvement in criminal activities. Grandmother Zaucha did not speak English, and because your dad was the oldest child, he assumed responsibility for taking care of your grandmother and the rearing of his younger siblings Ellen, Mary Jo, and Freddy. In his early childhood and youth, your father was also most likely involved in or influenced by his family's entanglement with organized crime."

Mom continued, "As you know, Ellen and her husband moved to California, perhaps to avoid being involved in the mob lifestyle. However, Mary Jo married a man connected to the Chicago underworld, and Freddy followed in his father's footsteps. Consequently, their children have been brought up under the same influences."

I remember that Aunt Ellen and my dad were very much alike; they both had a great sense of humor. I never heard my aunt discredit him, and she seemed to always be supportive of him. My aunt undoubtedly loved and appreciated Dad for taking care of her as a child and tried her best to be a positive influence on her brother…but to little avail.

Dad was forced to live surrounded by horrific, dark forces over which he had no control. He was the product of poverty and organized crime, and all the destruction and ruin they breed. Only in retrospect did I began to see how Dad became the person I knew him to be…a tough unyielding and emotionally hard person. One does what one learns. For my dad and his family, it was all about survival.

John Landesco, who was best known for his 1929 study entitled "Organized Crime in Chicago," helped me to understand through his writings what it means to be raised in an environment such as my dad's. His view was that every criminal career has its beginning and the problem of crime, in general, begins with the young people who were brought up in families involved in gang-related activities. These youths learn that if they got into trouble with the law, family and friends could get them out of trouble by perjury, bribery, and intimidation. Furthermore, it would be unlikely that anyone raised in such a background would become decent and law-abiding citizens.

Everywhere young kids looked, they saw lawlessness and vice. They watched hard-working fathers laboring for a few dollars but accumulating nothing, while the bootleggers and the gamblers rode around in expensive cars.

Sadly, these truthful words are still appropriate for today's youth. They speak about my father, and they also speak about me. I am the offspring of a man who learned as a child to be a bad character and example. To be clear, we did not come from a famous crime family. However, the Chicago Family influence had everything to do with what I became, even worse than Dad…a tough, unyielding, rigid, cold, heartless person.

The information passed down to me as a teenager should have given me clarity and understanding, but even as I heard the stories about my dad and his family, it never occurred to me that I was beginning to follow in their footsteps…just in a different way.

It has been said that you cannot hate someone you understand. I don't think I hated my dad. Perhaps there were moments when it felt like I did, but mostly I just hated his behavior, the things he did… the way he treated my mother and me. Understanding my family roots enabled me to eventually change the way I felt about my father, but the ultimate change in my relationship with my dad came after years of denial, confusion, and many wrong, terrible choices.

CHAPTER 2

POMONA PUNK

Life in the 1950s

I t was most likely soon after the Japanese bombed Pearl Harbor in 1941 that Dad was drafted into the Army. He was stationed at Fort Ord which was located in California. While serving his country, he met and married my mother, a California girl.

While Chicago, Illinois represented the past, Pomona, California represented the future. In the 1940s, movie production was brought to the small community of Pomona. It was used as a movie previewing location for major motion picture studios to see how their films would play to middle-class audiences around the country. The movie industry brought great affluence to the area and was viewed as the ideal place to live. Pomona was also where my dad chose to settle down and raise a family. WWII had ended, and he had been discharged from military service.

Living on the West Coast would keep him far away from "the family" influences in Chicago. Perhaps that is why Aunt Ellen and her family moved to Southern California. Aside from being comfortably removed from their old life in Chicago, they could live a respectable life and frequently visit her oldest brother, his wife and children, Mary Jo, Jimmy, Roy, and Ron…that would be me, the youngest. I was born in late 1953.

The 1950s was a period of time when the country was finally recovering from the Great Depression and the ravages of World War II. Like other parts of the country, Pomona was enjoying the beginning of an economic boom. Homeownership and the development of suburbs were becoming more common. Pomona promised a more prosperous lifestyle for young families.

Most upper and middle-class people love to reminisce about how great things were in the 1950s. It was a simple way of life when families lived in a house with at least three bedrooms, one phone and one black and white TV, which got three stations. There was one family car for everyone to share, and kids could get a driver's license at age fourteen, which I did. Most families respected God and went to church twice on Sunday and every Wednesday night. They valued their country, their teachers, their school and those in authority. But above all, they respected their elders.

It seemed there were no locks on doors, car keys were left in the car's ignition switch, and if someone lost their wallet, it would get returned. Children could play outside without fear of being kidnapped, ride their bikes all over the countryside, go to the public swimming pool and stay out all day if they wanted to. Clothes were conservative, and the mandatory, military draft made service a virtual certainty. Most young men proudly served their country because they loved America and what it stood for. The '50s were prosperous, and if you had a decent job, you couldn't ask for much more.

However, that particular decade was not such a good time unless you were white, male, and wealthy. It had its dark side, which is rarely discussed, or even remembered. Racial tensions were high. Not everyone was white, rich or even well off. And there were some, of all races, who found unseemly ways to get the money to buy the things they could not afford…to buy the things the rich, white kids had. The '50s set the stage for the way I would live in the future.

I only have brief glimpses of my early childhood. We lived in an area considered to be for poor, middle-class families. In those years, we were not aware of what class our family belonged to. Dad was a good provider as a machinist, and Mom found a way to help by cleaning houses and doing laundry. For the most part, she was a stay-at-home mom.

We lived in a small, suburban house, had a car, and shopped for our clothes at Goodwill Thrift Stores and Salvation Army. We ate lots of spaghetti. Peanut butter sandwiches and lettuce and bologna sandwiches were regular parts of our diet. Dad took us fishing, to the beach, the mountains, and Disneyland. We created our own toys out of rocks and sticks and built forts in abandoned fields. Life for us kids during that time was just about having fun. Dad and Mom did the best they knew for their young family.

Most of the kids who lived in my neighborhood hung out at our house. Having friends became an important part of my life and fueled a misguided need to have lots of friends in years to come. Back then, I trusted everyone. My mom loved to have my friends over and would feed as many as would show up. As we grew older we played basketball, baseball, lifted my dad's weights and took swings at his punching bag. And we sneaked a peek at his *Playboy* magazine collection when he wasn't around. My dad taught me how to box, and later in life I became a brown belt in karate.

We had very few material possessions, but it really didn't matter. I just recall it was a good time in my life. It was the positive aspect of being raised in the '50s and the upside of my Mom's and Dad's personalities as well as their relationship with each other and us kids. I cherish those fleeting, happy memories with my family. I have this great need to hang on to the knowledge that my childhood was not all bad. And it wasn't. But the problem with the few good memories I have of my childhood is they are overshadowed by so many painful ones.

For instance, instead of asking me to do something like a normal father would, Dad would slap me on the back of my head with his hand demanding something like, "Change the damn TV channel!" If I did not meet his expectations, he would yell, "What's wrong with you, anyway?" He seldom showed me kindness and respect. There were few words of praise or approval…no "I love you," or "I am proud of you." I now realize it was most likely the way Dad had been treated by his father, who had learned this behavior from his father. Consequently, it was the only way my dad knew how to handle me.

This is not an excuse, but a reason, that helps me to have some compassion for my dad. It takes a man of character, who acts responsibly in life, to be a father. I saw my dad as a man but not always as a father. Sadly, Dad's actions fueled anger within me, and I began to wonder, "What is wrong with me, anyway?" There was a huge part of me that did not want to have power over people like my dad had power over me.

As I moved toward adolescence, I began to feel left out and unimportant to my immediate family. It seemed the older kids got everything, and I got nothing. I resented having to wear my brother's hand-me-down clothes.

At school, I began to notice what others had that I did not have. Things bothered me that never bothered me before. I started to feel an emptiness inside I did not understand. When I was at home, I sensed my mom was struggling. I felt desperate to help her but didn't know how. My family seemed to be changing, but I did not know why.

My maternal grandparents, Verne and Mildred, became my lifeline during those young years. They were always going to church and often took me with them. They taught me about God and His great love for me through Jesus. I remember that my grandpa seldom got angry about anything, but especially not at me. In my young mind, he was Gentle Ben like the big, brown bear in the storybook, *Gentle Ben*. Grandpa and Grandma planted seeds of faith that would lie dormant in the soil of my soul for a very long time. They were a safe refuge for me, and I know they loved me very much. From them I learned kindness and that the world isn't such a terrible place.

CHAPTER 3

DYSFUNCTION JUNCTION

Adolescence

When I was a young boy, the term "dysfunctional family" didn't exist, but by today's definition it definitely applied to our family. We were the walking wounded but were clueless, even though each of us was acting out our pain in various ways. But I was the one who took the word dysfunctional to a very different level, and I have to wonder…just how is a kid supposed to sift through the sands of right and wrong when bad examples far outweigh the good ones… when bad seeds are planted in the soil of his soul. I don't think any child can, at any age. As I think back to my young years of innocence, I am faced with accepting some hard realities.

I recall a time when my dad was building a patio in our backyard. There was a business that sold bricks down the street from where we lived. One day Dad sent two of my friends and me over to "acquire" some of those bricks for his new patio. No problem. We took my Red

Ryder wagon and filled it with bricks. Dad rewarded us with bottles of Coke which, back then, was a rare treat. A few days later he asked us to repeat the drill. On the third trip, we got caught by the security guard, who promptly delivered me to my father. My friends ran away leaving me holding the goods alone. My dad was gracious to the security guard, but when he took me into the house, he patted me on the back and said, "Good job, Ron!"

I learned from my father the value of having double standards. You can do what you want until you get caught, and even then, there were no real consequences. You can't learn what is right when you are rewarded for doing wrong. Just like my father's family did in Chicago years before me. It was a generational thing. My dad learned from his father to look the other way when bribes and payoffs were commonplace to law enforcement and politicians. In other words, stealing bricks was no big deal. We kept the bricks and laughed it off.

Dad's stint in the Army only added to the tough guy image he had created for himself. Much like mob tactics, the army was about intimidation, which caused people to do things out of fear, even if they did not want to. It was either kick ass or get your ass kicked. Dad never had anyone to teach him otherwise, and he did not hesitate to pass that trait down to me.

I remember when I was thirteen-years-old my dad was driving home from work when he saw that two neighbor kids had jumped me and were beating the crap out of me. He stormed out of his car and pulled them off me. He then proceeded to throw them at me, one at a time, for me to fight. By the time I kicked both their asses and pinned both boys to the ground, they were covered in blood and so was I. Dad had given me a chance to kick ass, and I did just that. When we got home, my mother was horrified when she saw me. My father quickly exclaimed, "Now I have a reason to be proud of my son. My kid beat up two white boys!" He turned to me with a huge grin on his face, patted me on the back, and said, "That's my son!"

At the time, I thought he was out of his mind for allowing me to hurt someone so viciously. Even though I felt protected, I was confused and angry because I thought I was the badass I knew my father to be. I did not like that feeling. But those feelings were quickly challenged as seeds of wanting and needing power over people were being planted within me.

As I got older, it was not uncommon for Dad to take me to bars with him. It appeared to me he would purposely pick a fight with someone; he rarely lost a battle. Not until I was 50 years old did I realize how I had taken it all in and learned my lesson well.

I had a revealing visual experience as I was watching the movie, *Secondhand Lions*. I felt as though I was watching a scene from my own life. Robert Duvall played the part of an elderly uncle who unexpectedly became the caretaker for his young nephew. There is a bar scene in the movie in which some young punks decide to beat up the old man. Instead, the old man whipped all of them senseless, showing the young nephew how to get tough and take care of himself. That scared little boy was me watching my dad teaching me that fighting was a way of life that I needed to get used to. And I did.

Although Dad was instilling violence in me, he was also teaching me how to use that aggression to protect myself. He was showing me how to survive. I had a severe stuttering problem which made me a victim of bullying and ridicule. When I got excited or nervous and could not get my words out, people would tease me. I became so angry I would haul off and punch them. In his own way, I believe my father was testing me to see if I could actually take care of myself. The reality is that Dad probably saved my life many times later on. He had no way of knowing the extent of just how much I would need what he taught me as I became more reckless and out of control.

Of all the dark clouds that hang over my few good memories, the ones I have of my parents' chaotic relationship are the ones I wish I could forget. I vividly remember the times I witnessed my dad verbally and physically abusing my mom.

One day when my father was abusing my mother, I had had enough. I stood in front of my dad as he taunted me…laughing in my face. "What kind of punk do you think you are?" The rage and anger had built up so strong within me that I confidently shouted, "A punk that's about to stick you if you don't leave my mom alone!"

The switchblade I held in my hand waved back and forth as I pointed it directly at my dad. My body, unyielding and rigid, was ready to do whatever it took to force my father to back away from my mother. Mom stood scared and shivering as her abusive husband pinned her against the wall. I could hardly believe my eyes when Dad let go of her and slowly backed away from me.

On that particular day, I snapped. I could not and would not take it any longer. Between the age of thirteen and fourteen, I was almost as big as my dad. Perhaps my size is what made him back down, but I often wondered how that could be. My dad was afraid of no one. After all, since when can a child use a threat against a father that will cause the father to stop doing something so terrible? But that is what happened. Confronting my dad caused him to face the reality of what he was doing. He never physically abused my mother again.

That day I felt empowered. But I did not understand that having power over people would become both my friend and my enemy.

Dad was a heavy drinker and gambler who loved taking frequent jaunts to Las Vegas. Often he would get into the car and drive almost four hours away to enjoy all that Sin City[i] had to offer…the roll of the dice, the money, the women, the alcohol, the lifestyle. His habits eventually became addictions, which progressed as the years passed. On one of his many trips, he lost all his money and couldn't get home. My prideful father called my mother and asked her to send him money. Embarrassed, my mom, who often had to ask for financial help from her parents, did so once again.

In my early teens, Dad began taking me to Las Vegas with him. At first I thought it was cool because I was finally getting to go somewhere with my dad. It sounded exciting, but in reality going with him only fueled the deadly flame that was slowly growing within me. I did not like what I saw. I loved my dad, but I began to see that he was a bigot, a womanizer, a cheat and a real scoundrel. I have often wondered how my mother dealt with the pain of seeing my dad walk out the door with her teenage son, knowing exactly where he was taking me. What were they thinking? And why didn't Mom stop him? Perhaps he thought this would make a man out of me; maybe she felt powerless to stop him. Either way, as their child, I didn't understand their choices, which ended up having devastating consequences for me as I walked through my teen years on the way to manhood and beyond.

There was a deep yearning within me that vowed I would never be like my dad when I grew up. He was many things I was determined never to become. But those words would someday come back to bite me as I became more and more like him.

I am not sure when my mother began to have an affair. The truth is they both openly cheated on each other without much effort to hide what they were doing. To make matters worse, they would sometimes take me with them, leaving me in the car. I was not unwise and knew exactly what they were doing. I could not escape their actions as shame stamped its ugly mark on my heart. Rage and anger lurked just beneath the surface of my young, raw and tender emotions. With every encounter, the toxic flame within me grew a little bigger as my own life began to spin out of control.

I was never allowed to have a voice when it came to expressing any feelings. My mom's favorite saying was, "Put up and shut up!" What she meant was to just get over it and move on. If I tried to say anything she would just tell me she had been hurt too. She had no real voice either. She had to deny and stuff her feelings. It was from my mother I learned how to deny reality and stuff my feelings too.

On the one hand, Mom could be cold and insensitive. On the other, she was very loving and incredibly sacrificial when it came to her kids…especially for me. That was probably because of my stuttering problem and because my dad was so hard on me. Even as I got older, my mom tried her best to make life easier for me. Nevertheless, I still feel the pain of those years, even now. Abuse of any kind, at any age, can cause complicated and confusing behavior, and my actions embodied both and then some.

Because of my mother's Baptist upbringing and my dad's Catholic background, divorce was out of the question. However, they finally divorced when I was about sixteen. I was being pulled between two worlds… one being evil, the other being somewhat good. I was called into court and asked to choose between them, but I could not make that choice. I didn't know where I belonged because I didn't believe I fit in anywhere or that anyone cared about me.

I spiraled more and more out of control, but no one was paying attention. Mom was in denial about the emotional pain I was in. I felt life was hopeless and succumbed to the lie that my life had no value. On impulse, I decided to take a bottle of downers and check out altogether. My mother found me and called a friend to come help get me to the hospital. My stomach was pumped just in time to save my life.

When the divorce was final, Dad moved out of the house. My brother Roy and I stayed with Mom. Dad often returned trying to convince my mother to reconcile, which eventually she did. As sure as a leopard can't change its spots, my dad could not stop seeing other women. It didn't take long before he began to cheat on her again. But for Mom, enough was enough. They divorced for the second time before I turned eighteen.

Throughout all those years it had been my poor mother who had received the worst of my father's inexcusable behavior. It appears that their marriage actually crumbled even before it began. It was after the second divorce that Mom confided in me, "Ron, your father was like an animal on our wedding night. There was no love, just agonizing pain." I saw unbearable grief and sadness on her face as she confessed her secret to me. She was a virgin, had come from a good Christian home and had no idea, in truth, who the man was she married. It seems to me that one night of hell changed who my mother was and caused her to become a submissive, battered, broken, critical woman. Something within her died that night, and her life became controlled by her husband.

I felt sorrow and compassion for Mom because of all the years her heart had been broken by my own father. I found myself asking, "What kind of man would do this to a woman?" No man should ever disrespect, hit or harm a woman in any way and never ever use them as a sexual object. Once again, I swore I would never become like my father. I would never treat women as sexual objects. But those convictions and promises to myself would also come back to haunt me. I took the undeniable dysfunction of my father and internalized it as my own.

Looking back, I can hardly blame my mom for the affair or the divorce. It seems to me she was a shell of a woman who was trapped in a loveless, abusive marriage. Once her children became more independent and no longer needed her constant care, she lost her purpose for hanging on. Anger and humiliation stirred in the same pot for a long time will explode sooner or later. The affair was her outlet.

On the other hand, how can I put the sole blame on my dad, who was so young and had to grow up so fast? He had so much responsibility on his shoulders. He was never a child or a teenager; he missed out on those tender years. More importantly, he had no positive role models. He was a survivor who did the only thing he knew to do. I am not making excuses for my parents or their behavior, but when I apply reason to their out-of-control lives, it helps me to understand why they did the things they did to each other and to me.

For many years, I blamed myself for my parent's divorce because I had been such a difficult child. Situations escalated quickly when I was around because I was so hyperactive. My dad frequently yelled at me to calm down. My siblings were not high-strung, so I could not possibly blame them for the problems at home. By the time my parents divorced for the second time, I had created so much havoc in the family that I was convinced it was entirely my fault that my parents could not live together.

I had a behavioral and emotional disorder called Conduct Disorder[ii] (CD), which was not recognized until the late 1960s. Therefore, I did not have the benefit of being correctly diagnosed or receiving medication to help me. Nor did I get speech therapy to correct my constant stuttering. Perhaps if I had received help, things might have been different for my family and me, but in reality, it would not have changed who my parents were. Children imitate what they see, not necessarily what they are told. Parents sometimes give mixed messages. They say, "Don't drink", but kids often watch their parents get drunk. Parents tell kids not to do drugs, but then get high on drugs. Children who grow up with these kinds of mixed signals are often confused about what is right and what is wrong. I was clueless, and everyone around me was clueless, to the many factors in my life that were causing me to react in so many negative ways. The following quote from the book, *I Can Begin Again*,[iii] clearly defines my family, but it mostly defines me:

> "Every precious child is born innocent with the expectation of being loved, nurtured and protected. When a child's trust is broken by neglect, sexual, physical, emotional or spiritual abuse, the child will eventually find ways to compensate for the shame that has stolen their innocence. The resulting powerlessness will lead the child into a life of varied, often destructive, and unmanageable behaviors.

> "A dysfunctional family is created when unfavorable conditions interfere with the healthy structure of a family unit. Unresolved issues become monsters that refuse to go away. These monsters have long-term effects on the children/ adults who come from dysfunctional families in which any one of the following abusive conditions has occurred:

> "When children are disrespected and or shamed, the child feels worthless and insecure and as an adult becomes controlling of others. When unprotected, children will learn they have no boundaries and consequently often do not respect the boundaries of others. Anyone can do anything to them, and they will remain silent. But as adults, they often become filled with rage, anger, and resentments. When goodness is stolen, children believe they are bad and, as adults will often become rebellious and live in a world of denial. Reality becomes skewed. When their emotional and physical needs and wants are denied, they will often develop addiction issues or physical and mental issues. They will always be searching

for love and acceptance. And when innocence is thwarted, maturity is often delayed; emotional development progresses slowly. They will either exert no control of their lives, or they will try to control every facet of their lives, or they may even exhibit both of these traits simultaneously. Real intimacy will elude them, no matter what. When children are abused in any way, they are powerless to protect themselves from those who are entrusted to love and protect them."

Eventually, all my siblings broke away from the family influence, but I have no doubt their lives were deeply affected by our unhealthy home life. While my family's involvement with organized crime in Chicago had much to do with the shaping of my dad and me, my two brothers, Jimmy and Roy, managed to escape corruption's grip. My sister, Mary Jo, was sheltered by Dad and seemed much less affected than my brothers or me. Unfortunately, I was the one left to carry on the family legacy. I was, after all, my father's son.

It is essential for you, the reader, to understand how I managed to create so much chaos for my family and ultimately for myself. In the next few chapters, I will go back and let you experience those years with me. But be forewarned! I was not the ideal teenager.

CHAPTER 4

HIGH ON GOD AND HIGH ON DRUGS

The 1960s

As previously mentioned, my grandparents were the shelter in my stormy life. Going to the Baptist church with my grandparents was actually something I looked forward to. When I was in church with them, I would forget about my life at home. The smoldering flame of anger and rage that was burning inside me seemed to go out during those hours away from the things that threatened to turn the flame into a raging fire.

I loved attending the church services where I enjoyed Christian music and singing in the choir. I played on the church basketball team and was involved in most youth activities. I even asked Jesus to come into my life without fully understanding what that really meant. Nevertheless, I believed Jesus gave me the promise of eternal life, and I experienced His tender love for me.

As I think about what those experiences meant to me, I question how anyone can choose to walk away from light and goodness into darkness and evil? How does the darkness seem to swallow up the light so easily? Why does the light just go away and let the darkness have its way? Or does it? Why are the young and innocent so vulnerable and quickly attracted to the very things that have the potential to harm or destroy them? At the age of thirteen, these were questions I did not know to ask.

Tragically, I did not think I would ever walk away from my grandparents' godly values, and I could not imagine I would make the deadliest, life-changing choices of my life at such a young age. I had no idea the wounds of my childhood would lead me into dark, evil places. I would learn the hard way the bad decisions I made would ultimately make me. I would change into someone I could not recognize. Oh, how I wish I had asked the hard questions. Perhaps then, I might not have bought the cultural lies of the 1960s.

Sex, drugs, and rock 'n' roll describe the decade as one of reckless overindulgence and decay. The hippie generation sprang to life in the '60s. Hippies rejected the traditional social and political values of the culture and proclaimed a belief in universal peace and love, which is now referred to as "coexisting." They dressed unconventionally, lived communally, and were wild about their psychedelic drugs. I didn't dress or act like a hippie, but I welcomed their attitudes regarding free love, sex, and drugs into my life. Of course, in my twisted state of mind, I never thought of myself as strange and far-out like they were.

After the Beatles and British Invasion of 1964, rock music became like a god. San Francisco and Los Angeles were home to bands that have become legendary. The Grateful Dead, Jefferson Airplane, Big Brother and the Holding Company, The Doors, Quicksilver Messenger Service, Deep Purple, and the Steve Miller Band just to name a few. They all played in venues that have become almost as legendary as the bands themselves. These same clubs became places where British bands came, eager to crack into the American music scene. It was a time when anything could happen, and it often did. There were plenty of drugs, sex, and rock and roll music, and I wanted to partake in them all.

Our country's youth turned to the political left in early and mid-1960s, forging a counterculture that exists to this day. There was a significant increase in crime and urban unrest of all types. By the end of the decade, politicians campaigned on restoring law and order, and a conservative was elected president of our nation.

Looking back at this period of unrest in America, I can see how primed I was to be a part of its changing culture. I wanted all that it had to offer me, and I went for it hook, line and sinker. I was the perfect example of one who had negative, unstable role models. My life was becoming all about peer pressure and wanting more. I began to crave more of what others had that I did not have…the drugs, the money, the big house, the expensive cars, the girls and the sex. I wanted the thrill of being perceived as a "Superman" character and began to believe in the deception that I was that image. I started to embrace the demonic world that I was being tempted to live in.

It all began when I was fourteen. I can still recall how excited I was to see my twenty-year-old brother Jimmy return from Germany after serving in the Army. He and my other brother Roy shared an apartment-like room, which was detached from the house where I lived with my mom. At the time we lived in Westmont, California, a subdivision of Pomona located about an hour's drive northeast of San Diego and the Mexican border town of Tijuana, Mexico.

I was a young, impressionable teenager when Jimmy came home. I remember admiring posters taped on Jimmy's walls of Jimi Hendrix, Bob Dylan and other cool rock icons. I was clueless about the drug-filled, self-gratifying lifestyles these men led. And just as clueless to the risky choice I made when I accepted a joint and got wasted with my brother.

He probably thought it was funny watching his little brother get high. But for me, it was more than just fun. It was an escape. It was a way to feel so good about myself that I never wanted to come down from the fantasy world it created in my head. I wanted more...more freedom from the pain, turmoil, and confusion of my dysfunctional childhood.

Before long, I was doing drugs with my friends. I began taking reds and yellows (downers), whites, cross-tops and black beauties (speed) and eventually smoking more pot. Jimmy would sometimes turn off the lights in his room, turn on the strobe light, and play his harmonica. I would play my snare drums with him. It seemed to me we were just two brothers having a good time...a very *high*, good time. I embraced everything about this new way of life.

In the beginning, I never saw doing drugs as a bad thing. Back then schools did not have D.A.R.E. (Drug Abuse Resistance Education) to teach us otherwise. I was even clueless to the fact that using drugs was against the law. I just felt if my cool brother and my friends did drugs, I could too. I would be cool just like them. But I wasn't entirely clueless about the danger of doing drugs. I just did not want to admit it and hid my fears in that place called denial. In fact, I was given a huge warning sign that using illegal drugs to get high had real and severe consequences.

A friend invited me to go along with him to his friend's house to buy drugs. Right away his friend pulled out something unfamiliar to me. He called it a "kit," which consisted of a needle, rubber tourniquet, a spoon, and heroin. I quickly discovered this was the killer of all drugs. As this guy injected the heroin into his body, he literally went into cardiac arrest. He died right there on the spot...right in front of me. I was shocked and scared. I vowed to stay away from heroin, and I did.

One would think that witnessing the senseless, drug-induced death of a human being would have made me run the opposite direction as fast as I could, but not so. I stayed in total denial about what other illegal substances could do to me and chose to ignore the warning I was given. Addiction already had its grip on me, and my foolish pride gave me dangerous confidence. Life was all about me, and more was never enough to fill my empty soul. I became utterly determined to do what I wanted to do and when I wanted to do it. I would just be more careful than those other fools.

Because I was a big guy for my age, people were actually afraid of me and would not cross me. I had no regard for how my actions would adversely affect anyone else. I never thought about consequences nor did I seem to suffer because of them. I was too smart for my own good and was growing up too fast. Yet, I was too immature to even notice that I was going down a path that was taking many people, young and old, into a bottomless, dark pit where many would be lost forever. Once I stepped onto that path, nothing could stop me.

Beginning with just one joint, at a very young age, drugs controlled my life. From that time on, I don't remember doing much of anything without drugs being involved. As I moved through my teenage years and became deeper and deeper entrenched in the drug scene, I met more and more people who influenced my decision to continue on a destructive path. In fact, peer pressure was tremendous for me. I had a great need to fit in and to be better than all those "other" people. Not only did I want what they had, but I also wanted to have power over them, and to be more powerful than they were.

And so this is where it ended…the good, godly, and positive things in my life. I left it all behind and never looked back. I became a different person. I replaced the natural high of God with a much different, unnatural kind of high. Because of circumstances in my life and the use of drugs, the church was no longer the lifeline I wanted.

CHAPTER 5

PEER PRESSURES

My Troubled Teens

Young people are vulnerable to peer pressure. By the time I was in the ninth grade, I had several jobs, owned my own car, and I thought I was "Joe Bitchin'." I had a big ego and, like most other teens, I wanted to be noticed and accepted. I tried to fit in, especially with the rich kids. My peers wanted drugs, and I became the one who could make the deal. I always thought the people I dealt with were my friends, but instead I just paid a high price to be accepted by people who really did not care about me at all.

I often hung out with a guy I will identify as Mick. We would go to his apartment and get high together. However, I thought it was really cool when we went to Mick's father's house to get high because his father was a prominent political figure in the city of Pomona. Once while driving around in my van, I had a horrifying LSD trip. I began to hallucinate and see skulls, skeletons and all kinds of scary images. I was absolutely terrified because I could not make a distinction between what was real and what was only in my head.

Mick suggested we go to his dad's house where I could come down. I was surprised when his dad got involved in helping me come out of my drug-induced trip. To my knowledge, this influential man never told anyone about what I had done. Instead of thinking about my welfare, it seemed to me that his actions were motivated by the need to protect his political position as well as the need to shield his son. It is important to understand peer pressure is not limited to young people. Adults are often just as easily swayed by their position in life, and their friends enable this behavior.

I recall going to a block party in Hollywood Hills where a friend's parents lived. There was plenty of acid to go around; in fact, I remember seeing trash cans filled with LSD. As I tell this story, I find it hard to believe that I was just a young adult, only 19 years old, and I was the one providing the "blow" (cocaine). No one seemed to care what people were doing, and no one called the cops.

Now that I think about it, I can only imagine what would have happened if an uninvited neighbor had appeared and challenged what was going on. No doubt everyone at the party would have been arrested and the party shut down, but the concerned citizen would have been rejected and ruined socially throughout the neighborhood. Peer pressure, even among adults, will cause the upper-class society to think twice about interfering and doing what is right for fear of rejection and isolation.

My values were being shaped by those whom I chose to be around…young and middle-aged adults, as well as my self-indulgent peers. I could not see the truth about the life I was seeking. I could not even comprehend how life could or should be lived any differently. I didn't even know what a good, moral life looked like.

My desire to impress others became my goal in life. I had a need to keep up an image and to meet or exceed others' expectations. I wanted to be "The Man," so I made sure everyone knew I was in control and the right guy to know. Being considered the right guy wasn't about being right or wrong. It was about making an impression, even if I had to break the law, which I often did just to get attention.

There were many times when I encouraged others to make wrong choices with me. As my bad behavior became bigger than life, I became more efficient at learning how to manipulate people and influence them. I was actually using peer pressure in the same way it was using me. It was a never-ending, vicious cycle.

Being tall, blonde and good-looking made it easy to hang out with guys who were older than me and easy to influence those who were my own age or younger. I even manipulated a young neighbor girl into letting me have my first sexual experience with her. This behavior toward the opposite sex would only escalate with intensity as I got older. I was blind to the fact that I was becoming just like my father…or worse.

Committing crimes became my partner right along with my use of drugs and the need to impress my peers, especially the chicks. Doing a crime was mostly about the thrill of having power and control over others and, of course, not getting caught. It started with petty offenses, which soon became boring. I convinced my friends to move up in the world of crime. Don't be deceived. It was the drugs that gave me the courage to go down a slippery slope to do bigger and more challenging jobs by going into wealthy neighborhoods. We needed money to buy drugs, so we began breaking into homes where we stole coin collections, power tools, stereos and anything of value. I became a felon at a very young age.

For years my friends and I never got caught. But one night when my brother was with us, we were in the middle of stealing tires off a car. Suddenly, I felt a sharp knife pressed against my throat. I heard a loud voice in my ear demanding, "Freeze!" We all stopped dead-still in our tracks! A rather large man informed us he had called the cops. Somehow, I managed to convince the guy to give us a fighting chance to run, and we'd all just forget the whole thing and never bother him again. And run we did! We successfully dodged the bright beams of light coming from the Halo (helicopter) in search of us. I am still dumbfounded the man actually trusted me and let us run away. But that is just an example of the kind of power I had over people, and I ate it up like candy. Or should I say like "coke?"

I perpetuated taking drugs because of peer pressure and my need to escape reality. But as time passed my motivation became more twisted and complicated. I befriended Will, who was a year behind me in school. He was a smooth talker and the kind of guy who could convince a used car salesman into buying his own car. Eventually, Will introduced me to many in his circle of drug users and dealers; he had solid connections to well-connected sources. I was seventeen when I made the deadly leap into the dark world of dealing/selling drugs.

As time progressed, we got hash oil and hashish smuggled in from Germany and Afghanistan. Later, we got into LSD, Orange Sunshine, Purple Haze and Microdot. One of the dealers, Steven, brought us the best quality stuff from Vietnam.

I even acquired a large shipment of drugs from a guy named Timothy Leary, a Harvard professor, psychologist, and writer. He was known for encouraging the study of and developing the use of psychedelic drugs, specifically LSD, for therapeutic reasons under controlled conditions. One of the ways he did this was by getting his students to participate in the studies. During the 1960s and 1970s, he was arrested often enough to see the inside of 36 different prisons worldwide and was considered to be one of the most dangerous men in America. I'm sure it wasn't just because of the drugs or thumbing his nose at authority; Leary encouraged the younger generation to "tune in, turn on, and drop out."

Just to emphasize how crazy and mixed up I was during the time I was dealing drugs, I was also earning "honest" money. I worked at a car wash, a gas station, the school store, and I did yard work. There were a lot of good things I learned from Mom, but one of the most important was the value of a dollar and how to make it stretch. This knowledge was useful to me as I learned to manage the business of drug dealing. It helped me to achieve the success I craved.

I know I keep calling attention to peer pressure, but I need to stress the importance of understanding how dangerous peer pressure is. My internal sense of value in the world came from how others viewed me. I quickly learned how to say the right things to the right people at the right time depending on the circumstances at the moment. I became the product of peer expectations. When my peers were supporting my evil actions and criminal lifestyle, they were actually encouraging me to self-destruct. The lens through which others saw me came entirely from the wrong perspective. Throughout my teenage years, my thinking changed more and more into a corrupt state. I deceived myself into believing I was seeking the good life. I didn't know what the good life really looked like without being judged as "not cool" or "goody-goody." I just sought to be a really cool dude in the eyes of my peers. That was all that really mattered to me.

Outwardly, I appeared to be an average kid. My image was intact, and no one in school suspected what I was doing behind the scenes. I had a job in the school store which enabled me to interact with a lot of different students. I participated in gymnastics and played basketball. I also worked in the school office and got to know the chief counselor, Cathy Wilson. She was married to the head of parking lot security, Willie Wilson, who had a brief stint with the Detroit Lions in the National Football League and later became a career policeman. As crazy as this may sound, he actually had a very positive influence on my life. He planted good seeds within me that would eventually help me to survive.

However, evil has a subtle way of creeping into one's life. As the Bible teaches, bad company corrupts good morals, and I was well on my way to keeping terrible company. After all, doing drugs and being corrupt is no respecter of persons…rich, poor, young, old, black, white, or brown. My high school years in Pomona brought many changes in my life, including a lot of racial violence, which had a significant impact on my life.

The 1960s was a decade of battles between whites and blacks. Conservative whites demanded segregation, especially in the Deep South. Consequently, blacks were not allowed to share water fountains, schools or public restrooms with whites. Black citizens just wanted to be treated equally, and blacks who bravely served in wars and military duty only wanted to be treated fairly. I was just too young, macho, and stupid to understand any of this. It was a very different time in America.

I am not making excuses for my behavior, but as I tell my story, it will help you understand my deplorable actions against blacks. I don't think I could have escaped following in the unfortunate footsteps of other young, white kids considering the American culture war between black and white people, peer pressure, and my family.

My dad and those in my extended family were very prejudiced against African Americans, especially Uncle Freddy. His son, Freddy Jr., who claimed to be a black belt in karate, held the same biases as his father and was a dangerous influence on me when I was younger. One day when they were visiting us in California, Freddy Jr. and I were riding around in the car. We drove by four black teens walking down the street minding their own business. I paid no attention to them, but suddenly I heard my cousin yell, "Stop the car!" I didn't have a clue what was about to happen. I pumped the brakes, and in a flash, my cousin jumped out of the car. I watched in stunned silence as he beat the crap out of them. When Freddy Jr. got back in the car, he answered the look of disbelief on my face, "Ron, from where I come from those black kids don't walk on the street. WE DO!" I snapped back with, "Hey Dude, you don't do that stuff out here in California. You're going to get us busted."

I can still hear the raw and bitter hate in my cousin's voice. I had never before witnessed an outright attack on someone because of the color of their skin. I did not understand why, but this outrageous act against these innocent kids really bothered me. My own mind and heart had not yet been seared and hardened like others in my family. But more bad seeds were planted within me that day. It was not long until my own attitude began to change. It is hard to admit that I became even more toxic than my cousin.

An interesting side story to this incident is another example of my Chicago family's *I can get by with anything* attitude. On one of their visits, my Uncle Freddy tried to bribe a California patrolman with a $100 bill when he got pulled over for speeding. The officer just reminded my uncle he was in California, not Chicago, and told him to put his money away. My uncle then handed him three $100 bills. Ignoring the green bucks, the cop issued him a ticket and told him to go back to Chicago. In Chicago, our family knew the cops and got by with just about anything.

In what many historians dubbed "The Great Migration," segregated blacks made their way to California from the southern states after World War II. Many were relocated to Pomona, California, where I went to high school. My friend Will came up with the word "sponge," (start prevention of n*****s getting everything) which was the code-word used to alert white guys to join a brawl against black kids who started school fights with freedom from any form of consequences. Authorities were too afraid to enforce punishment to blacks in the wake of The Civil Rights Act of 1964. We saw that any wrongdoing done by a black kid did not seem to result in the same set of consequences we white kids faced. Perhaps it was overcompensation for years of inexcusable oppression.

For the most part, the black youth of my generation were always trying to avoid trouble because of how the race card was used against them. However, that did not stop the fighting and development of gangs. I remember those same groups of people were always beating the crap out of my friends. Enemy lines were drawn, and both sides started to fight back.

I was a senior in high school, and my friend Will was in the eleventh grade when we fought back against a rival gang. A friend of ours had recently gotten his teeth knocked out, and we were pissed off. It all started when we were smoking hash from a hookah in Will's garage. A terrified neighborhood kid ran into the garage shouting that he was being chased.

"Let's get those n******s!!" Will yelled. We sent out two guys as decoys to intentionally lure the black kids back down the street away from Will's garage. The plan was for the rest of us to come up behind them with baseball bats in our hands and start swinging. Not only were they outnumbered but they were also ill-equipped.

Thud! Thud! Thud!

In drumbeat rhythm was the sound of baseball bats hitting heads, backs, arms, and legs. We swung our bats at the four black boys, who appeared to be our own ages. I struck with all the anger and raging fury of one who had no conscience, no heart, and no soul. I heard the cruel sound in my ears…the sound of bones cracking. I saw the blood, dripping, splattering in every direction. I smelled their fear as it hung thick in the night air. But I could not smell my own fear. I was numb.

We beat those boys senseless and were damn proud of it. Proud of the fact that we finally took a stand and made them pay. But we made one big mistake. During the fight, mine and Will's names were thoughtlessly called out, and our victims heard and remembered them. Word quickly got out at school who was responsible for nearly beating those kids to death. It took no time for our opposition to recruit the Black Panthers who alleged they were going to kill all of us. We let it be known that we wanted to "get it on" and would meet them at Sam's house to settle things once and for all.

We were ignorant and arrogant. We knew nothing about how powerful and dangerous the Panthers were. Likewise, they did not realize how cocky and high we were. Each of us gathered friends from our own neighborhoods and instructed them to bring as many shotguns, rifles, and Molotov cocktails they could find. We were armed like a guerrilla army as we positioned ourselves on the rooftops and behind bushes. We waited without fear and were eager for action. It was a dark night; the moon was faint.

As an unfamiliar car crept slowly down the street where Sam lived, several of us jumped out of the bushes with shotguns drawn. We pumped our guns and stuck them in the driver's face demanding, "Where is the rest of your gang?" Tensions mounted as their dark eyes began to see the outline of human figures appear brandishing a vast arsenal of weapons. The Panthers were ordered to leave and return with the rest of their gang. We set out to make a lasting impression, and we did. They knew we were dead serious and wasted no time speeding away. They never came back, so we figured they were not the real Black Panthers after all. Now that I think about it, had they been the real deal they never would have left in the first place… and we'd probably all be dead.

To celebrate our victory, we partied until early in the morning and got totally wasted. Three of our friends got stopped on the way home and were arrested by the local police, probably more because of the guns in their car than for being high. They suffered the consequences of their actions by being sent to a reform school. They were not allowed to return to their regular high school, which ultimately became a positive thing for each of them. One of them even became a sheriff. In retrospect, I wish I had also been caught. Being sent away from my peers might have turned my life around and kept me from self-destructing.

After the shotgun incident surfaced, the vice principal of my high school, Mr. Everett, called me into his office. He got right to the point and confronted me about my involvement. I lied and told him I had nothing to do with it. Knowing I was lying, he called me on it. I replied the only way I knew how to…with rebellious anger.

"You don't know sh*t," I yelled disrespectfully.

Picking up a sheet of paper from his desk, he haughtily replied, "Either way, you have enough credits to graduate, so here is your diploma. You are now graduated."

I couldn't believe what I had just heard. If looks could kill, the man would have died on the spot.

"Who in the f**** is going to protect my friends?" I asked.

"You do not need to be concerned about that," he replied with apparent disdain.

I snatched the diploma out of his hand and walked out of his office. I could feel the smoldering flame within me intensify as I stormed out of the building.

A few months later, I was shocked when got a phone call from the school administrator offering me a job as School Monitor. I thought it was a joke! Silently, I questioned what I was being told—I am being given the responsibility for keeping order and watching out for violent behavior on the school campus—really? But it was not a joke, and I gladly took the job.

The security guard, Willie Wilson, whom I mentioned earlier, became my boss. He treated me like a son, and I looked up to him as my black dad. Willie tried to teach me about forgiving others and the importance of respecting race and people in general. He also helped me accept that there are good and bad people in every race. In my eyes, Willie was an honorable man among men. I will be forever thankful to him for being there for me. It was the ironies of all ironies considering how I had treated people of his race. I have often wondered if he knew about my secret life on campus.

Although my job was to keep peace at the school, I used it to my advantage. My newfound influence made me the most popular guy on campus. During those years I became a pro at using threats of fear and intimidation to further whatever I wanted, whenever I wanted it. I had the perfect forum to sell drugs and get laid. Because I drove a Porsche, I was a chick-magnet with lots of power. I could get girls hall passes any-time they needed one, and I could trade drugs for sex anytime I wanted.

What a trip to think about me, of all people, being offered a posi-tion that required the monitoring of bad behavior. The school gave a low-life guy like me power, which I fully abused. And the '60s gave me all the right tools and contacts to become precisely what I wanted to become. A successful "businessman" and a thriving, badass drug dealer! The leader of my peers! An essential player!

I don't recall my parents ever discussing, or even questioning, what was going on in my life. It is all too ridiculous to even think about.

CHAPTER 6

LIFE IN THE FAST LANE

The 1970s

The '70s were a continuation of the '60s, only faster and more outrageous. It was a confused, rebellious, and riotous decade. African-Americans, Native Americans, gays, and lesbians continued their fight for equality while many Americans protested against the ongoing war in Vietnam. Social and cultural changes in the '60s became more accepted as normal in the "Me Decade." Americans were slowly becoming more sensitive to racial issues, and many believed rights and privileges should be enjoyed by all American citizens and not just one race.

Long hair and outrageous clothing became the norm for people of all backgrounds. It was a trend-laden, fad-happy decade. Sex outside of traditional marriage became widely practiced and accepted by the younger generation, whose values were reshaped by the popular culture. They went to wife-swapping parties, and drug use increased and became even more accepted. They used their hard-fought freedom to do as they pleased, to wear what they wanted, to grow their hair long, to have no-strings-attached sex, and do excessive amounts of drugs. Their freedom, in other words, was intensely personal.

The decade also seemed like a repeat of the 1960s in the political arena as well. A traditional political movement, referred to as "The Right," arose with the 1968 election of Richard Milhous Nixon and declared a commitment to traditional religion, patriotism, and smaller, less interfering government. The movement organized people to take action to defend political conservatism, traditional family roles, and less spending by Uncle Sam (the government). By the end of the decade, the divisions and disappointments between the "Right" and the "Left" had set a tone for public life that many would argue is still with us today.

As time shifted from my teenage years into my twenties, I became the living, breathing embodiment of the '70s. I was all about sex, drugs, and rock and roll. My life was all about partying, having fun, hanging out with the guys, and developing a successful career as a drug dealer. I sold pot, cocaine, acid, uppers, downers, and PCP (angel dust) to students and middle-aged men and women. Of course, the women preferred to offer up sex rather than to pay money, and I was more than happy to accommodate them. My conscience became more and more hardened. I had no boundaries, nor did I respect the boundaries of others. It terrifies me to realize how insensitive I was to the warnings all around me about the toxic trip I was on and how self-important and self-absorbed I was.

I know it is hard to believe, but I actually enrolled in a community college in Southern California. Never mind that it took me six years to graduate, and as you will discover, I was a busy young man during those six years. A lot happened, and your head will be swimming as you try to keep up with me. Sometimes even my head gets a little dizzy trying to sort it all out. So, let's get started.

Like a skilled pro, I took my "business" to college with me. I got a job as the campus mailman, which gave me visibility and much exposure on campus. It also gave me opportunities to make money. I had a custom van with a bed in the back, which became a place to sell drugs, get high, and of course, have sex with my non-cash paying customers.

I majored in Business Management with a minor in Photography. My degree plan was perfect for me because it taught me how to better manage my career as a drug dealer. I learned how to keep books and records and manage collections.

During my college years and beyond, my ego continued to be fed by more sex, drugs, and rock and roll…everything that money could buy. I had plenty of cash to spend. I personally owned Porsches and drove my friends' cars, which included Ferraris, Rolls Royce, Lamborghinis, a Lotus, and other high-end vehicles like the Mercedes-Benz. This was the lifestyle I had desperately yearned for. It was the good life I wanted. I thought I was so damn cool!

"Let's make a deal!" was the phrase drug dealers loved to hear. My favorite was "taking care of *bizness*" because it was all about selling drugs and getting rich. Whether it was making a deal or doing business, when it came to drugs, there were rules to follow. The most important one was to always take care of your accounts receivable. I would go out with my other so-called friends to ensure customers paid their "bills" in a timely fashion. In fact, "collection" was a common occurrence. Believe me, we kept good records and had no hesitation when it came to collecting what was owed us.

I was incredibly resourceful when it came to instilling fear and terrorizing my customers if they did not pay up. I discovered with power brought across convincingly, there would never be a need for violence. Otherwise, there is no doubt in my mind extreme violence, and possibly murder, would have entered the equation. Of course, I was prepared for anything and was always ready to instill fear with my two best friends: Smith & Wesson.

It is impossible to count the number of times I pulled my gun on a "client" just to persuade him to pay what he owed me for drugs. I could have cared less where it happened, either in a nightclub or in a client's home, or just out in the open public. When it came time to collect, I didn't mess around. Everyone knew I was crazy enough that I might just off them if they did not pay up.

On one occasion I went with my friend Dan to Colorado to sell two kilos of cocaine to members of a famous rock band called The Eagles. On the way, we stopped at a rest area, and while Dan was in the restroom, I noticed a few Mexican guys walking straight towards our car. I pulled my two guns from the shoulder harness I was wearing and stammered, "V-vamanos or else I w-ill s-shoot you!" It is almost comical to think how fast those guys stopped in their tracks, turned around, and ran like crazy.

This incident only confirms just how powerful I was and how terrified people were of me. Not only did I look like a hostile force—I *was* a hostile force. One look into my stone-cold eyes and no one wanted to mess with me. Those guys quickly chose not to challenge me because of the fear I held over them, and I did not mind using that power, with limits, to get the job done. I didn't want to shoot anyone, and I sure did not want anyone to shoot me. Deep down there was still a thread of goodness in me that could override my own lack of moral judgment. But that virtue—that ounce of goodness was slowly vanishing.

One night Will and I were in Walter Mitty's Bar in Pomona. We were listening to the then undiscovered Van Halen band, which later became our first rock band customer. That was the night we decided to become *bizness* partners. Will was the perfect guy to help me reach the over-the-top success that I hungered for. I wanted him on my side because he could always get the "stuff" we needed. As a result, our friendship and partnership were sealed, and together we exceeded our expectations in the world of drug dealing.

To help our *bizness* grow, I contacted our friend, Dan, who had a connection with a man who had direct drug ties with Timothy Leary and the Brotherhood, a group of drug smugglers who had links to Hollywood and other high places. Dan lived in Laguna Beach, the hub for drug smuggling in Southern California in the 1970s. His connection got us the very best quality drugs available. We were undoubtedly one of the major California players back then because we could supply quality cocaine that no one else could get. It was considered to be some of the best "blow" around at the time.

Will contacted his friend, Sam, who had contacts in a favorite Huntington Beach nightclub called the Golden Bear. Many successful rock bands started out performing there including Janis Joplin, Neil Young, The Flying Burrito Brothers, and Seal & Craft. Sam was another primary source for high-quality drugs as was Doug, a Vietnam veteran. When Doug first returned from Nam, he brought back precious stones to sell but eventually graduated to smuggling some of the best Southeast Asian dope to be found.

As my drug career advanced, trafficking became an even more significant part of my life. Doing *bizness* with these heavy-duty dealers involved getting truckloads of bales of marijuana and kegs of hash oil brought in from Mexico by way of Brownsville, Texas.

We made frequent trips to Mexico, via Tijuana, to smuggle drugs. We filled spare tires in cars and the inside panels of our vans with kilos of marijuana and cocaine. We stuffed surfboards with drugs and placed them on top of the vans. Wearing our swim trunks and flip-flops, we drove through the border checkpoint appearing to be the perfect surfer dudes with our bikini-clad chicks out to have fun. We declared that we were just going to Ensenada, Mexico, to surf and catch some waves. The border authorities never suspected us, and without fail allowed us entrance into their country. Fortunately for us, all of this happened long before drug-sniffing dogs and high-tech surveillance equipment were on the scene.

Hussong's Cantina in Ensenada was the place to go. It was a major hangout for many San Diego State University students who wanted to blow off some steam and party. We made a huge bundle of cash off those rich kids.

If I had ever gotten caught for drug smuggling, I'd still be in a Mexican jail or dead. I don't even like to think about two horrific days I actually spent in one of those jails. On one of my smuggling trips, I woke up with no memory of how I landed in that Mexican hellhole. It was not uncommon for me to get so drunk or stoned I could not recall what I had been doing the night before. When my eyes opened, I was lying on the ground. The cell had a dirt floor and in the corner of the cell was a hole, which served as a toilet. They gave me something they called food, which I would not eat, and I cannot find words to describe how utterly filthy the place was.

As reality began to sink in, I knew I was in a dangerous place. I was terrified of the other men in the cell. Frozen with fear, I hardly moved a muscle the whole time because I was afraid for my life. Instinctively I knew my tough-guy attitude was of no use to me. I even tried to hunker down to look smaller. To this day I don't know how it happened, and I don't know how much it cost, but my friends showed up and got me out of that vile place.

During this period of time, I had an associate who lived in Newport Beach, California. Even though he owned a successful construction company, he envied my lifestyle so much he became involved in the *bizness*. He bought an airplane to smuggle cocaine and other drugs from South America to Florida[iv] for the cartel. He even had associates who were involved with the Colombian Cartel led by Pablo Escobar, the wealthiest and most powerful drug kingpin of them all. He would tell me stories of just how crazy the cocaine biz was in South America. Totally insane and gruesome stuff went on that I can't disclose…but just imagine the worst!

Another of my associates was a very influential man from Florida who had judges, lawyers, and cops in his pocket. I recall a somewhat humorous story about this man when he was once doing a drug deal in San Clemente, California. He was on the beach with a prostitute when he passed out after taking Quaaludes. After curfew, police were cruising the beach for vagrants and found him wearing only the prostitute's pantyhose. He was arrested, but after one quick phone call, he was out of jail within 24 hours. This guy made so much money that once, without realizing it, he left a briefcase with $200,000 cash on the roof of his car and drove off. It is alleged that he just shrugged his shoulders and said, "Oh well. There is plenty more where that came from."

I often got downers that were confiscated from cops during drug busts in exchange for pot. Corruption in law enforcement was well-known and accepted. When I found out that a cop friend, who held the world weightlifting record for squat lifting, had sex with a sixteen-year-old girl, all I could see was pure evil. They ended up getting married after she graduated from high school. All that I can say now is that what he did was illegal then and still is today. Nevertheless, I remember being outright disgusted by what my friend did…even though I committed far worse sins. I was blind to my own evil deception and in denial about my own life. I don't know how much more hypocritical a person can get, but a drug-filled mind will screw up the way you think about everything.

I began this chapter with the fast lane of the 70s. I warned you that a lot was going on during the six years it took me to finish college, and I invited you to join me as I sorted through parts of my life during that time. However, we have only scratched the surface. Let's continue. There was much more craziness going on in my life in the fast lane of the 70s.

CHAPTER 7

MAUI, MARRIAGE, AND MADNESS

I met Rick in my college photography class. Even though he was older than me, we became friends. He taught me a lot about how to take and develop pictures. After he graduated from college, Rick moved to Maui, Hawaii. We kept in touch, and eventually he invited me to come to Maui to help him build a house in the jungle. I took him up on his offer and made a temporary move to Hawaii. Rick worked at the once famous Pineapple Hill Restaurant which was frequented by rock stars. This was, in fact, where my cocaine business started in Hawaii.

In the 70s Maui was akin to the American Wild West from 1865-1895. It was undeveloped, untamed, and an entirely different place than it is now. Drug deals went down in bars, clubs and in plain sight of the general public. In fact, drugs were handled so openly that it was evident that law enforcement was on the take.

Rick knew many people on Maui, and he bought a lot of drugs from me, which was incredibly profitable. One of our friends in Lahaina was friends with Willie K, a well-known musician in Hawaii and the mainland. We did our share of partying together and had a lot of good times. (I recently ran into Willie K, and he now has a family and has cleaned up his life. I am so proud of him and still love his music.)

While I mostly supplied the cocaine, Rick and other associates sold drugs to members of Fleetwood Mac, Van Halen, The Eagles, Crosby, Stills, Nash and Young, Joe Walsh, Dave Mason, James Taylor, Eric Clapton and too many more to mention. They also sold drugs to movie stars as well as judges, lawyers, cops and prominent business-men. When it came to cocaine, addiction is no respecter of persons or line of work.

Leading executives in the recording industry not only used drugs but supplied them for profit to rock stars signed under their label. For the record, Stevie Nicks, Glenn Frey, David Crosby, James Taylor, Eric Clapton, Robin Williams, and Eddie Van Halen have talked openly about their lifelong addictions after they made a vow to get sober. Guitarist Joe Walsh from the James Gang Rock Band, and now with The Eagles, had a saying that seemed appropriate for the times, "I only got drunk once, but it lasted twenty years!" They all loved coming to Hawaii for their drugs and to party, but they were also careful not to get caught by using drug mules—people who transports illegal drugs by concealing them in their bodies, employees, and friends to carry their drugs for them.

I started smuggling drugs on commercial air flights to Canada and Maui from California. The 1978 movie *Midnight Express* is based on a true story about an American student who was arrested for attempting to smuggle hash out of Turkey. From that movie I got the idea that I could tape cocaine to my body and smuggle it into Hawaii and Canada. I often traveled with my guns and marijuana packed in my checked suitcase and cocaine taped to my body. I also carried a gun in my otherwise empty Halliburton briefcase, which made me appear to be a prominent businessman.

Fast forwarding to the 1980s for a short story, Eagles co-founder Glenn Frey wrote a popular song called "Smuggler's Blues," which had a great effect on the popular TV series "Miami Vice." Watching the cutting-edge show was not only highly entertaining but gave me ideas for new ways to improve my business. Sometimes when I traveled between Hawaii and the mainland, I wore shorts, a Hawaiian shirt, and sandals. Taking a cue from Frey and others on the television series, I nailed the part of the perfect drug smuggler. No one paid much attention to me, and I was never suspected of doing anything illegal. I was even given the nickname "Maui Vice" by the local dealers.

If I had been caught smuggling drugs across an international border, I probably would have been put in the slammer for life. However, thinking I would suffer consequences for what I did was never a concern for me. Denial was the name of the game I played; it was a self-survival mechanism.

Continuing with the 70s…when I was in Hawaii, I usually stayed at Rick's remote place in the jungle, which was in Kahakuloa, Maui. It was an oasis in the jungle…at least half the time. During the day it was like the Garden of Eden, but at night it was a scary place because scorpions, wild boars, and bugs were everywhere. Routinely we went into surrounding towns at night to deal drugs. After doing business and all the bars closed, we would head back to Rick's pad in the jungle. The roads leading to his place were not paved, and there were no lights to help guide the way. Rick drove his four-wheel drive as far as he could with nothing but his off-road lights on. He parked at the edge of Kahakuloa village, and then we hiked into the jungle. At two o'clock in the morning, it was pitch black, but I was too strung out to be afraid something would happen to me. It was our sanctuary and our safety zone. We were very much aware if people knew where to find us they might possibly kill us and take our drugs.

Maui had a vast, corrupt drug trade. Even ex-drug enforcement agents were on the take. I personally knew of agents who said they would keep the marijuana that was supposed to be burned. I once felt sorry for them because I thought these guys risked their lives and got paid squat, but then I discovered that half of them were on the take. I felt a bit prideful in the fact I still earned about four times what they did and lived the "good" life.

It was rumored that the Japanese Mafia ran the state, but the Chief of Police and his relatives enforced their wishes. Many beat their wives, drank alcohol excessively, and often went on sexual escapades with young girls for weeks at a time. They were utterly corrupt because of their greedy love of money. How ironic I could only judge others' greed, but I could not see my own.

In downtown Lahaina, Longhi's Restaurant was the main hangout for all the rock stars. Other favorite places were Moose McGillycuddy's, Kimo's, Lahaina Broiler, Whales Tale, and Pioneer Inn. The Blue Max was the music venue where most of them performed and where Rick and my drug-dealing days exploded on Maui. The nightlife was absolutely insane. Plenty of loose women roamed the bars, and cocaine was better than cash to purchase their favors.

The marijuana we sold in Hawaii was known as "Maui Wowie," and it more than lived up to its nickname. This is what I smuggled from Maui and sold in California.

When I was in California, I kept it in mason jars. When the jar was opened, the quality was so intense that the scent was like an overpowering perfume in contrast to the typical low-grade street pot most of my associates sold.

Even though I spent a lot of time in Hawaii, I actually resided in California where I continued to work on my college degree. Students would gather to smoke pot on a green patch of grass, which Will and I nicknamed "Hollywood and Vine." One day while Will and I were lounging on the grassy area, I noticed a stunning girl walking across the campus. She was medium height, had long, brown, wavy hair and a full figured body that sent my lust-filled mind reeling. I handed my joint to Will and ran after her. Determined to meet this girl, I finally found her in one of the hallways. At first she didn't want to have anything to do with me, but eventually I won her over. Consequently, drugs were not the only thing that impacted my life while living in the fast lane of the 70s.

This sweet young lady named Rhonda walked into my life on February 14, 1977. Not only was Rhonda beautiful on the outside but she had a purity and innocence I had not experienced. She came from a Christian home and had been sheltered from the evils of this world. I think it was her naivety that made her so vulnerable to the evil that lurked within me. As I recall, it was actually Will who offered Rhonda her first hit of cocaine. I like to think I had no part in pulling her into the dark pit of drug addiction, but I was there, and I did not stop him or her. Guilt haunts me as I remember with regret the past I cannot change.

Rhonda and I fell in love. I was so captivated by her that I wanted to spend the rest of my life with her. I asked Rhonda to marry me in May 1977, and we were married December 3 of that same year. Her parents gave her the perfect wedding every girl dreams of. But even before we exchanged vows, I was unfaithful to her, and on our wedding day, I proved my unworthiness. I left the well-attended reception, which was held at San Dimas Country Club in Southern California, to go outside and get high with my friends.

My evil addictions overpowered my love for this loving, kind woman. It is difficult to admit that very soon after I said my marriage vows to Rhonda, I was unfaithful. I knew the life I lived and craved was too dangerous for her to be around, and I loved her too much to hurt her any more than I already had. I had to ask my beautiful bride to leave me for her own well-being. She knew she would never be able to compete with my desire for drugs, and she knew I would not give them up. Rhonda talked to her father about the situation, and he advised her it would be best if we had our marriage annulled. We separated one year to the day after we met, on February 14, 1978. Our marriage was annulled in July 1979. I was powerless to change who I had become or my way of life…not even for her.

By the end of the decade, my business was growing like wildfire, and I was making money hand-over-fist. American culture was becoming increasingly uglier, and I was changing right along with it. My heart was seared and hardened to the core of my being. My moral compass eroded to the point that I had lost all dignity and had absolutely no regard for human life.

Many crazy, scary things happened along the way toward my total and complete moral decay. I can't fit these stories into the timeline of my life because they are random memories that I have. When your mind is controlled by drugs, time gets lost. Following are few of those stories. And by the way, there are many more stories to tell, but I would really be insane to write about most of them.

I went to a construction site to collect from a client. When I got there, the client was standing outside on scaffolding. Scarcely acknowledging my presences, he told me to f*** off. I demanded, "If I have to go up there, it won't be to talk, and you won't like where you land. Come on down and let's finish our *bizness,* and I'll be on my way."

By then the fiery flame that burned inside me was out of control. I didn't care about this man's life. I just wanted what was mine. When he hesitated, I began to attack the tall, wooden platform he was standing on. Blind, raging anger almost drove me to kill the guy, and he knew it. He wasted no time coming down and paying for the drugs he had previously purchased from me.

I recall another time when a high-profile customer kept putting me off about paying his bill. He played in a famous band and was accustomed to his peers catering to him. I knew he was staying in a local hotel, so I decided to pay him a visit. He undoubtedly did not know who he was messing with because he made all kinds of excuses for delaying payment. He might have had a huge ego, but he was a runt of a man. I bent over, grabbed him by his ankles, picked him up, and walked out to the balcony where I hung him by his heels over the railing.

Suddenly, he was staring upside down at the street six stories below him. Kicking wildly, he began to scream and holler, promising he would pay up if I would pull him back over the rail. Just for reassurance—and a bit of fun—I removed my hand from one of his legs. Pretending to drop him, I said, "OOPS!!" I am sure he thought he was going to die. Terrified, he promised immediate payment along with his Rolex watch and all of his electronic equipment.

Satisfied that I had made a lasting impression, I graciously agreed to spare the man's life. I collected my loot and left the hotel a happy drug dealer. I am almost positive he had to change his underwear when I left. As you read this story, I am sure you are laughing. It is a bit comical. However, I am horrified to think that I might have accidentally dropped the man.

My no-nonsense reputation followed me. Nobody wanted to mess with Ron Zaucha, and for a good reason…he was crazy.

When it came to the *bizness* of dealing drugs, I knew many people involved in the trade were crazy and utterly out of their drug-filled minds. Drug deals were often made in seedy motel rooms. A friend and I were waiting for such a deal to happen when we heard a strange, somewhat familiar sound coming from the room next to us. We looked at each other in disbelief as we tried to process what we were hearing.

My words hardly faltered, "W-w-what does that sound like to y-y-you?"

My friend said, "It sounds like a chainsaw to me."

Without giving it another thought, I yelled, "L-let's get the hell out of h-h-here!"

We did not hang around and wait for the deal to happen. With our hearts pounding in our chests, we grabbed our stuff and split as fast as we could. I was smart enough not to mix words or screw around with someone crazier than I was.

Having a drug-filled mind will make anyone lose their mind. There were times when I would black out after getting into a fight. As I've already said, I never wanted to get into something that would get another human being or me killed. However, there were times when I would instinctively react to a situation and not think. I can't count the number of times I would wake up fearful because I was never sure if I had killed someone or not. If my dad had not taught me survival skills as a young boy, I would not be alive today.

To truly understand the drug culture of the '70s and how it affected me, I recommend you watch the movies *Scarface*, starring Al Pacino, and *Blow*, starring Johnny Depp. Be aware that these movies do not make the *bizness* look glamorious.

CHAPTER 8

THE BEGINNING OF THE END

The 1980s

As the 1980s emerged, the hippies were replaced by the yuppies. While the hippies had been mostly concerned about social issues and having a good time, the yuppies were all about the money. They were young, educated professionals who enjoyed the finer things in life.

"Greed Is Good" became the mantra of the '80s and was rewarded on many levels. The pleasure-seeking, self-indulging, self-gratifying, self-denial attitudes of the '60s and '70s were being re-evaluated. Drugs, which were once considered recreational, were now being revealed as addictive, deadly substances. As reports of celebrities entering drug rehab centers and the horrors of drug-ridden inner cities became widely known, First Lady Nancy Reagan's message to "Just Say No" to drugs became more influential. However, newer and more dangerous substances like crack cocaine made America's drug problem worse.

Hopeful dreams of the past had been worn down. In response, many Americans, especially evangelical Christians, embraced a new social, economic and political life. It was time for a change, not just in America, but also in Ron Zaucha.

I began to realize the people I associated with were even more insane and dangerous than I ever was. Anxiety and worry started to get a frightening grip on me. Drug dealers were obsessed with money and cared less and less about loyalty or friendship. They would not hesitate to screw you or rip you off. Self-seeking greed had taken over, and death was merely a part of doing business. To make matters worse, I did not trust the people around me and feared no one would have my back if something should go wrong. I can honestly say that I was loyal to my associates, and I would never rip them off. If I owed money, I would pay it. If I was owed money, I expected to be paid. It was just that simple. But there was a fine line to walk if there was a breakdown in my expectations. The possibility of what I might have done if that happened still haunts me.

The life I was living in Maui deteriorated so much that I was losing money instead of making money. That's because I broke the cardinal rule of dealing: Don't get high on your own supply. I was continuously stoned out of my mind, and paranoia began to overwhelm me. I got to the point I couldn't go anywhere without having a gun or two on me at all times. I was so obsessed that I kept a cocked pistol in my hand and under my pillow when I slept. More than once a gun went off in my hand while I was asleep. I am still amazed that a bullet never hit anyone, especially me.

I spent most of the '80s floating between Hawaii and the Mainland, foolishly squandering my life and my money. Finally, in 1988, I decided to completely break away from all my drug-dealing associates. I also began to accept I had a severe drug addiction when I actually stopped selling dope and increased my already excessive use of them. Money was not coming in, just going out. I made the decision to leave Maui for good and return to California.

I settled in La Verne, where I lived in a small mobile home and sunk as low as a human can go. Desperate to find relief from my demons, I would read the Bible my grandmother gave me for Christmas in 1980, while repeatedly getting high on acid, Quaaludes, cocaine, pot, alcohol, or any combination of them. I would often consume a fifth of whiskey all at once. I was so afraid I would get busted that I would flush my coke down the toilet and immediately regret it and then go buy more. And all the while I kept reading the Bible. I lost touch with reality as I fell deeper into the bottomless pit, I now realize, God had been trying so hard to keep me out of.

For many years I had an off-and-on relationship with a sexy woman named Teri. She was actually the one I allowed to come between me and the only woman I truly loved, my ex-wife, Rhonda. Teri was also the one who eventually became the catalyst that led me to my own downfall.

Since my life was about nothing but drugs and sex, there were times when Teri and I would go on three-day drug and sex binges. We'd snort lots of cocaine, down booze and Quaaludes, all of which doubled as aphrodisiacs. This led to having perverted sex until we passed out. She did things that made me crazy because her behavior was so erotic. It was even scary for me at times. But I could not stop seeing her. Our relationship was like being strapped together on a moving roller coaster from which neither of us could escape. I wanted to be free of her, but I needed her to satisfy my sexual addiction, even though her actions increased my paranoia. I thought I was in love with her, but in reality, I had an insatiable lust that consumed me… a craving so extreme that not even Teri was enough to satisfy. I would pay big money to have one or more call-girls at a time. But even that was not enough for my out of control sexual addiction.

On December 28, 1989, I was reading my Bible and desperately searching for answers. I began to reminisce about going to church with my grandparents and the joy I had once felt there as a young boy. Suddenly, the words I had been reading in the Bible seemed to be speaking to me. I found myself frantically pleading with God, "I don't know if you are real, but if you are really who you say you are, I beg you to show me and help me get out of the mess I have made of my life." Sometimes God has a strange way of answering our prayers.

That night my drug-induced paranoia persuaded me Teri was cheating on me. I decided to check up on her. When I drove by her house, I saw a car parked in front of her house that belonged to Tim, a fellow drug dealer. Enraged, I went back home, got my shotgun, and returned to Teri's house. With no feelings of wrongdoing, I literally destroyed Tim's car by pumping it full of ammo. Feeling vindicated, I somehow managed to drive back to my mobile home, where I sat feeling like King Kong…mighty, powerful, and unstoppable. I got even more loaded and more delusional. I reloaded my shotgun and went back to blast Tim's car for the second time.

When I arrived, the cops were already there. I saw Teri on the front porch pointing to me as I drove by. Instantly, the police were in their cars chasing after me. Because I knew the area so well, I was able to dodge them by driving through alleys and side streets. I thought I had ditched them, but my alcohol-driven mind foolishly told me I would be safe at home.

As I pulled into my driveway, four armed police officers jumped in front of me yelling, "Get out of the car!" The ignition of my SAAB 900 was on the floorboard. I put one hand up but reached down with the other one to turn off the ignition, which just happened to be where my shotgun was. It is a miracle the police didn't shoot me on the spot. A detective later told me they almost did.

I was hauled down to the Pomona police station, booked, and placed into a cell where I spent the next three days. I made a phone call to my friend John, who bailed me out. It was New Year's Eve 1989. John drove me back to my place where I knew my old and faithful friend would be waiting for us. We pulled out a bag of cocaine and celebrated. There was nothing to worry about. No shame. No remorse. No guilt. It was all good as long as I had something put up my nose.

PHOTO SECTION

My maternal grandparents, Verne and Mildred Fink, on their wedding day. These wonderful people gave me a safe haven and refuge from my dysfunctional home and introduced me to the Lord as a child. Their Godly influence helped shaped the man I am today.

My parents, Walt and Gladys Zaucha, on their wedding day. I wish I could say this was in happier times but my mother's admission to me years about that day later painted a different picture.

That's me in my first grade photo, looking pretty dapper in my suspenders. Even though I looked the part, I was not a great student.

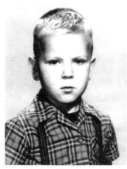

A collage of photos of me in my adolescence, including candid shots of me with my parents.

Top photo: A family photo that includes my parents and my three siblings – Roger, Margie, and John. Bottom photo: The Zaucha family visiting with the donkeys at Knotts Berry Farm, circa late 1950s.

That's clean cut teen is me when I was about 16 and already knee-deep in trouble. I dove into the deep end and stayed there.

A pictorial of my wayward youth and early twenties, tooling around Pomona, California, where I first started in the drug trade.

My expensive sports cars, which helped keep me in the fast lane. Fast cars and women were my downfall.

Left photo: This A-framed pre-fab home was flown in by helicopter in the middle of the jungle, which was our Hawaii hideout. Right photo: Me in Oahu, looking a little skinny. No doubt from dipping into my own supply.

Rhonda was the love of my life, and drugs blinded me to where I let her slip away.

Best man at a 1970s wedding. He supplied the party favors that night, which kept us fueled for the next few days.

My connections ultimately brought me fame and failure. My motto back then was "If you wanna play, you gotta pay."

After a stint in county jail, I literally saw the light – Jesus in a life-changing vision. That night led ultimately led me to a decision to follow Christ. On the left, that's my graduation day Vision International University. On the right I'm with Pastor Chuck Singleton, who gave me my first paying job in the ministry.

Wally Nelson (on the right), was a key figure in my Christian walk. He showed me what it took to run a ministry and how to walk the talk.

IF I GET TO CO
HOME WILL YOU READ
THIS BIBLE TO ME,

After I led my father to the Lord in which we were healed from our past, he wrote this heartwarming letter from the hospital bed, asking me to read him the Bible if he came home. He died the following day, but now he's with Jesus.

Hanging out with my mother after appearing on TBN. You can see from the photo, we had great affection for one another. She was my rock and biggest cheerleader.

Me preaching the word to about a crowd of a hundred people at the California Institution for Women. Prison ministry is the foundation of what I do and is like that old military phrase: many are called but few are chosen.

CHAPTER 9

HYPOCRITE WITH A CODE

The 1990s

Some will say the '90s was the happiest decade of our American lifetime. Peace, prosperity, and order were vibrant and healthy. Were there real problems in the 1990s? Of course, there were, but most Americans were happy to remain blissfully ignorant about them. Times indeed had changed in America, in the world, and for me, Ron Zaucha. I could no longer continue to be blissfully ignorant about my own disgraceful way of life.

A few weeks into the New Year I went to my arraignment. I was charged with shooting an unoccupied vehicle within the city limits and felt lucky the unpleasant incident was considered a misdemeanor. After my court appearance, I called a couple of cop friends and asked for their advice. The consensus was to fight the case because there were no witnesses.

When I asked Teri if she was going to press charges against me in court, she promised not to take sides. Tim had left town in fear of any vengeance from me. When I went to my first court appearance, I was caught off guard. Teri was present and had turned state's witness against me.

Foolishly, I called her on the phone and told her point blank, "If you go to court against me, I will take you to the Mojave Desert, and they will find you in pieces."

She told me I had nothing to worry about. I believed her. When I went to my next court appearance, I was re-arrested for threatening to kill her.

Even in my sinful, wicked state of being, I had been going to Central Baptist Church with Mom before and after my first arrest. Her pastor, Mark Nymeyer, who was also a Pomona City Councilman, attended all of my court hearings with Rhonda and my mother. Even now, I find it difficult to understand how my ex-wife could stand by me after the terrible ways I treated her. She still cared about me even though I was completely undeserving of any kindness from her. Throughout my court appearances, I had a public defender. Their job is pretty much to find a way to plea bargain and not mount a case because they are usually working pro bono. By God's grace, after I was found guilty but not yet sentenced, Rhonda paid for a lawyer to represent me just before sentencing.

I followed the advice of my cop friends to plead not guilty and fought the case. Teri continued to be the state's star witness, and through her testimony, I was found guilty. I was taken to Los Angeles County Jail. When I returned for sentencing, the attorney pleaded with the judge that this was my first offense and the decision of three years of jail time was harsh and uncalled for. The judge reconsidered and reconvened court at a later date. I was returned to the L.A. County Jail, which we called the "Zoo" because it was like being caged with a bunch of gorillas. I was later transferred to a super-maximum security facility called Wayside in Valencia, California.

I could hardly believe what was happening to me and was sure the authorities were out to nail me. Deep down inside, I understood that every criminal knows their number will come up sooner or later, and this was my time.

Being locked up in jail was terrifying. While at Wayside, my bunkie, a large African American male, told me all the men were *watching* me, but he would take care of me. I am convinced he was an angel because no one bothered me. But I still had to remain vigilant and watch my back.

One day when I was waiting in the chow line to be served a meal, an inmate walked up to me and got right in my face. He told me he didn't like my looks. I just stared back at him, spit in my hands, rubbed them together, and then combed my fingers through my hair.

"Is that better?" I said.

I did not take my eyes off him or crack a smile. I just stood there looking as serious as a rattlesnake about to strike. But I knew any minute we could "get it on."

"Are you trying to be a smart ass?" he yelled back.

Once again, I spit in my hands, ran my fingers through my hair and said, "Do I look any better now?"

Now highly agitated, the inmate shouted, "What is your problem, you piece of s***?"

I sternly replied, "I don't have a problem with you. I don't know you, and you don't know me. I will tell you my name and where I live. You give me your name and where you live."

We exchanged our jail cell addresses.

"Now, you know where I live, and I know where you live. So, we know each other. If you want to come visit me, you know I will f*** you up, and you will do the same to me. I am sure we both have plenty of enemies in this place already so why not just be friends instead?"

He looked at me in utter disbelief, shook his head and said, "Man you are weird!"

I offered my hand for him to shake. He grabbed my hand, gave it a quick shake, and walked away mumbling. And that was the end of that because nobody messed with Ron Zaucha.

That incident defined who I thought I was. Big! Tough! Cold-hearted! Powerful! But, in truth, I was scared to death! Satan, the evil one, had used the power of fear over people through me. I had been possessed by this dark spirit of fear. But now that same evil spirit was beginning to release fear into me. For the first time in my crime-filled life, I was consumed by fear.

While in jail I ran into an old roommate named Mike, who had been a bouncer in a club in Pomona called Moonshine where I use to drink. He was one of my former drug dealers. I recalled that he had once cold-cocked me over a drug deal gone south and knocked me out. When I came to, I got up off the floor, went for my gun and told him he was moving out of my house right then…one way or the other. He moved out. Mike wanted to be my friend in prison, but I ignored him. I was fearful of anyone in that place I could not trust, and there was no way I was going to trust that man. He never approached me again.

One day while in maximum security I was taking a nap. When I woke up, my shoes had literally been untied and taken off my feet. I was in shock but mostly frightened to realize how slick the men on my floor were. I decided from that day forward I needed to sleep with one eye open. Fear was chasing the one whose fear once chased others.

Two things are most hated in prison: a snitch and a thief. I wanted nothing to do with either of them. One day one of my bunkies stole my stuff...candy, money, writing paper, pencils, etc. It may not sound like much, but when you're in prison, it's all you have. I caught him red-handed and decided to set him up. I asked him if I could borrow a pencil and some paper from him. He was standing there with my property in his hands.

I said, "That looks familiar. I believe that belongs to me. Before I leave this place, I am going to make sure everyone here knows you are a thief. You'd better watch your back."

How ironic that I could see how despicable others were, but I remained blind to my own faults and sins. I find it hard to admit that I was such a hypocrite...a hypocrite with a code.

CHAPTER 10

THE VISION

A few of months after entering Wayside, I was lying on the top bunk bed with my eyes closed. Feeling depressed and hopeless, I was at the end of my rope. I had hit rock bottom.

Suddenly, I opened my eyes and appearing on the ceiling above me was the image of a man looking down at me. I was so startled I almost wet my pants. With my heart pounding against my chest and my hands clutching the sides of my narrow bed, I closed my eyes hoping this *thing* would go away. I opened my eyes again. The image was still there. I was afraid to move; there seemed to be no air in my lungs. I forced myself to look away, trying to convince myself that I was just dreaming or having a hallucination. Terrified, I rubbed my eyes and looked again, but nothing changed. I kept repeating my actions again and again, but the man would not go away.

I finally stopped struggling and slowly looked back at the ceiling, examining the details of the figure just a few feet above my head. The man appeared only from the chest up and seemed so real…alive. He had dark skin, piercing, dark blue eyes, long, wavy, brown hair, and a long, brown beard. He was wearing a white garment, and there was a bright, glowing light all around him. I was not convinced that what I was seeing was real. I blinked my eyes several more times, but the vision remained and the eyes, yes, it was the eyes. They were intense… looking into my soul, calling me, persuading me. My eyes locked with his and then…I knew I was not dreaming.

I began to tremble uncontrollably. I had learned to rule over my stuttering, but as I tried to speak, I could not manage my broken words.

"W-w-wha-a, w-w-wha-a-, w-w-ha-a, d-d-do-o y-y-yo-o-u w-wa-a-nt?"

The man spoke with tenderness, "Ron, I want you."

I thought…could this be Jesus?

It was as though he could read my mind.

I cannot explain it, but suddenly I knew that it was Jesus.

I felt confused.

"H-how c-could y-you w-want me? The life I've l-lived, the p-people I've hurt. I h-have t-totally rejected you? I've s-shamed m-myself, my family. Everything I h-have done has been e-evil? H-how could y-you w-want me? I-I am a t-terrible, terrible person. W-w-why?"

His answer was convicting, "I know who you are. I have seen what you have done. Ron, it is for those just like you that I came into this world. I came for the sick, not the well, and you are sick in your soul."

I began to feel a strong urge to give up everything that was important to me and to surrender everything to Jesus, including my life.

When I was finally able to find my voice, I spoke clearly and deliberately, "Jesus, if you really want me, I am yours. I give you my life. I will try to follow you."

As quickly as Jesus appeared, he disappeared, and I realized I was at peace for the first time in my life. I did not want to move; I could not move. Something deep within me changed as I felt a love I had never felt before. For a while, I remained suspended in what I now believe to be a Holy space of time. I had seen Jesus. I heard His voice call to me. My prayer had been answered, and somehow I knew He was going to do something about the mess I had made out of my life.

Even though there were at least sixty men all around me, no one saw Jesus but me. The next day, when it came my time to use the phone, I called my mother and told her I had seen and talked to Jesus. Her response was not surprising, "Ron, are you high again?"

I could not help but laugh, "N-no, Mom, n-not this time. Jesus really did appear to me, and I can't wait to tell you about it. I want to be in church on Easter and get resurrected like Jesus was. I want to change my life! Please Mom, will you call Grandma and ask her to bail me out of jail?" My mother was speechless, and I can only imagine the time of praise and thanksgiving she had when she hung up the phone.

She called Grandma, who agreed to pay a sizeable amount of her own money to pay the bondsman's fee. She then called Rhonda, and the two of them went to my mobile home and got rid of all my drug paraphernalia. They had already sold my truck, my boat, and all the expensive things I had purchased with my drug money to pay my bills while I was in prison.

For the first time in my life, I felt deep, unrelenting shame. I did not deserve their unconditional love. They were the perfect examples of Jesus to me, and I will always be grateful to God for Mom, Rhonda, and my grandparents. I realize how fortunate I am because not everyone has someone to stand by and help them.

On Easter Sunday, April 15, 1990, I went to church with Mom. I had no doubt that I was in church that morning because God had answered her prayers and the prayers of many others. When Pastor Mark Nymeyer asked if anyone in the congregation wanted to come forward and kneel at the altar and pray to receive Jesus Christ as their

Lord and Savior, I went forward and fell face down on the floor. I began bawling like a baby and could not stop.

When I finally got up off the floor, I said the sinner's prayer. I was 37 years old when I asked Jesus to be Lord and Savior of my life. When I did, I was immediately delivered from my decades-long drug addiction. I felt as though a thousand pound weight had been lifted off my shoulders. From that moment on, I became a changed man, and by the grace of God, I have continued to grow and change every day. I continually give praise to Jesus for instantly delivering me.

It was on Mom's birthday that I had to appear in court for my sentencing. With the help of Rhonda's lawyer, the judge allowed me to say a few words before sentencing.

"Your Honor, I have become a Christian, and I must tell the truth. I stand before you a guilty man." I explained the events surrounding the crime I was about to be sentenced for and pleaded guilty as charged.

The judge hesitated a long time before he finally responded, "Son, I think you have lost your mind."

I tried to give him clarity, "No, Your Honor, I actually found it when I received Jesus as my Lord and Savior. Whatever happens is in God's hands."

His response was, "I still think you are crazy! I am going to send you to Chino Men's Prison for observation."

CHAPTER 11

LOCKDOWN

I have not written about the many times I was put in jail during my younger years for doing stupid things. I once felt lucky I always managed to get released without suffering severe consequences. I now realize I was not lucky at all and deserved to be sternly punished. In fact, I should have been sent to reform school. Nevertheless, my knowledge about jail life began at a very young age, but as a foolish kid, I had no clue how dangerous long-term prison time is or that I would one day experience it firsthand.

Before sharing the details of my time in prison, I will recap some of the events of chapters 8 and 9 for clarification. When I was arrested for the last time on December 28, 1989, I was in complete denial about how serious my situation was. Like my Chicago family, I thought I could get by with anything. My first reality check was when the arresting officers relentlessly beat me because they thought I was reaching for a shotgun on the floorboard of my car. By 1 a.m. I was locked up in a jail cell where I spent the next seventy-two hours. When I appeared for arraignment, Teri, had turned state's evidence on me for threatening to kill her. I was found guilty and was sent to a series of jails to await sentencing. At sentencing, the judge sent me to Chino Men's Prison for evaluation. After returning from Chino, I received my final sentencing.

I was first sent to the Los Angeles County Jail to await sentencing. Long before I spent time there, I had heard horror stories about the place. It had a reputation for being the largest and worst jail system in the United States and continues to hold claim to that status today. It was overcrowded and filthy. In fact, it was disgusting. The food was disgusting, and you were lucky if you saw one hour of sunshine a day. It was a place where men were frequently raped and murdered. I found out fast that gangs ran the jail, and I had to figure out who the gang members were and how to avoid getting into an altercation with any of them.

I was assigned to 9500 Block where seventy-to-eighty hardened criminals were being housed in one large room. It was a place waiting for disaster to happen. Inmates did things to play with your head and caused you to get angry and react. They would steal from you, ridicule you, and demand you join in their gangs with threats and intimidations. I could never allow myself to close both eyes to rest or sleep.

While in the L.A. County jail, I experienced bone-chilling fear. It was even worse than what I had experience in the Mexico jail as a teenager. I was terrified to take a shower because I had been warned that if someone really wanted to rape me, they would. Because of my size, experience, and my own threatening demeanor, I stood my ground the first time a man told me what he wanted to do with me. I let him know exactly what I would do to him if he touched me. The inmate walked away and did not bother me again.

My worst day in the L.A. jail was when I witnessed a gang rape and murder no less than fifteen feet away from me. From that time forward I was a changed man. Fear controlled me like never before. I mentally wrapped myself in a cocoon of self-protection and relied on the toughness I learned from my dad to survive. I was called "pecker-wood," which is a term that originated as a racial slur against whites, but in prison, it is used to refer to white inmates in general or to identify white gang members.

I also spent a few months of time in Wayside Detention Center which had super-maximum security. The worst of the worst resided there. They had to force extra control, and lockdowns were everyday occurrences. The *Yard*, an enclosed outside area, was a place where makeshift knives (shivs) and razors were passed around and used on inmates. I was deeply relieved when I was moved out of that terrifying place.

It was four in the morning when I began my trip to Chino Men's Prison. Chains were placed around my waist, ankles, and hands. The chain around my waist was then connected to the chain around the waist of the man behind me, who was chained to the man behind him, etc. I was connected to 70 men while being processed out of my jail unit. I could not walk; I could only shuffle my feet to move around. Once I was on the bus, I was chained to the bar in front of the seat… too bad if I had to go to the bathroom. The bus made numerous stops to pick up other inmates. Before arriving at Chino, fourteen hours later, the bus driver warned me to stay out of the weight pile because a man who looked like me was killed there the day before. And guess what? I never went close to the weight pile. From then on, every turn I took became more terrifying than the last.

Upon arrival, the busload of linked-together-men shuffled to a gym-like room to wait for processing. Even though there was row after row of bunk beds, sleep was impossible. Bright lights remained on, and there never was a moment of silence. When I finally got to the processing area, I felt as though I was part of a herd of cattle with no identity

– degraded to nothing. All dignity was stolen as every orifice on my body was violated.

"Bend over," the processing officer demanded.

"You can't fit in there!" I defiantly mouthed back to him.

The uniformed man kicked me so hard in my butt that I flew into the air. I decided right then that I needed to keep my big mouth shut.

I was housed in Otay Dorm with about 80 other men. It was a large room with bunk beds stacked together like sardines in a can… up one narrow aisle and down another. There was never any time to be alone. It was never quiet. It was never peaceful. It was never safe. It was a place where survival was almost impossible, and it was exhausting. As they say, it is what it is…and you can't do nothin' about it!

Chino was much like the jails I had already been in, but with one exception: they allowed Christian ministries to come into the prison. They also provided time and space for Christians and inmates who were Christ-followers to meet together. Inmates seeking to know about Jesus were also invited to these meetings.

I was a very new Christian when I entered Chino. I began attending evening prayer meetings which were led by a man named John. It was there I started to see the hand of God working in my life. I was slowly being changed from being self-centered to being Christ-centered, and I began to place the needs of others above my own needs. During these sessions, I started to see miracles that God worked through the faith-filled prayers of these men. On a personal note, my mom asked us to pray for my brother's son David, who had a brain tumor. Our group of men prayed for David, and he was healed. This made such a great impression on me that I began to seek God more and more. As a result, God gave me a deep hunger to learn more about prayer. Through my experiences with John and these men, my eyes were opened to so many new truths about God. My mind was no longer being hardened with lies from the enemy of my soul, Satan. It was being renewed by the Word of God and by the work of the Holy Spirit in my life.

While at Chino two volunteer chaplains helped me understand what it meant to be a genuine Christian. I had a lot to learn. One of them, Les Warren, baptized me outside in a freezing cold horse trough. I said to him, "Oh my God, the old man froze to death!"

Laughing, Les replied, "Well, it does not matter as long as the *old man* is dead,"[1] The other Chaplin, Marlin Baker, gave me a Bible, which I still have to this day. Little did I know that years later I would meet Wally Nelson, a friend of Marlin's, who would have an enormous impact on my life.

I had been sent to Chino so that my mental state could be evaluated by counselors and psychiatrists. Throughout my time there I never got angry or upset with the doctors during any of my sessions. One of the counselors noticed this about me and at one of my sessions commented, "Ron, you never seem to be angry. Why aren't you angry about being in prison or angry about what got you here in the first place?"

"I don't need to get angry or be angry about anything," I said.

"Well, what does make you angry?" he asked.

"Nothing!" I replied.

"Well, what used to make you angry?" he probed.

"People like you!"

Appearing not to be offended the man continued, "Tell me in your own words your story. How did you end up here? What brought you to Chino?"

And so I told him my story. He sat behind his desk in deep thought for a long time. Without a hint of emotion, he finally declared, "You're

---

1 2 Corinthians 5:17 Therefore, if anyone is in Christ, he is a new creature; the old has gone, the new has come. Romans 6:6 For we know that our old self was crucified with Jesus so that the body of sin might be done away with.

not crazy, you're just plain stupid." He stamped Not Prison Material on the official paperwork and immediately sent me back to LA.

Arrangements were made for me to reappear in court for final sentencing. I was not sure what the decision would be, but I was prepared to accept whatever verdict was about to be handed down to me. I knew that I deserved the worst penalty possible. Standing calmly before the judge, I had the feeling that not only did he remember me, he was also struggling to find just the right words to say to me. Finally, he took a hard look into my eyes and said with resolve, "I guess I was right. You really aren't crazy after all! I am sentencing you to one year in county jail instead of three."

There are no words to describe that moment for me. For the first time in my life I felt humble. I knew with every fiber of my being that it was only by God's grace and mercy that I was only going to spend one year in prison for threatening to kill Terri. But even more humbling was the knowledge that I deserved to spend the rest of my life doing time for *all* the other things I did, but I knew I never would. On August 30, 1990, because of time already served, I left prison early because of good behavior.

The suit I had worn the day I was sentenced was nowhere to be found. The old Ron would have gotten angry and threatened bodily harm. Instead, I just said, "No problem." I walked out the door into a new life wearing my prison clothes; for the first time, humility walked beside me.

Being at my mom's house after leaving prison reminded me of how grateful I was for the smallest of things. Mom fixed me the best meal I'd had in a year, and I appreciated her more than words can say. I cherished having my own private bathroom, with no one watching or sitting next to me, and having a big comfortable bed to sleep in. Best of all, there was no one sleeping anywhere near me. My first night at home I slept like a baby. I could hardly wait for my new life to begin.

CHAPTER 12

MY WILDERNESS JOURNEY

I had cautious expectations about what my born-again Christian life would be like. The life I once knew was behind me. I was a new man with a bright future ahead of me. I expected that life as a Christian would be a bed of roses without any thorns. I was confident everyone would accept me, love me, and give me a chance to be the changed man I had become. I have already established that I am not one to learn things the easy way and some things just never change. I had a lot to learn.

It was important for me to break ties with my past. The first thing on my list was to call all my former associates and my so-called friends and tell them to never call me or get in touch with me again, for any reason…except one. I wanted them to find what I had found. I boldly explained how I had become a Christian and how Jesus had changed my life. I tried in the best way I knew to give them a chance to learn about Jesus, His love, and His forgiveness.

I told them, "If you decide you want to have what I have then call me, and we will talk about it." I wasn't exactly surprised when I had few takers. I only heard back from three men, and I helped each of them get off drugs and led all of them to faith in Jesus.

On my second day out of prison, I went to see my probation officer (PO) as I was instructed to report directly to him within 48 hours after my release. He was a stern, no-nonsense character. He cautioned me not to violate my probation and gave me the rules I had to follow to stay out of trouble. His orders were relatively simple: No guns. No drugs. No contacts with any felons. Get a job. Go to meetings.

I told him I didn't need to go to meetings because I had been delivered from my drug addiction. He mockingly laughed and said, "I have lost count of how many men have told me that before." I actually laughed too, but was thinking…not me!

He continued, "The best thing you can do for yourself is to do as I say and to make my job as easy as possible. Do that, and we will get along just fine! Come back and see me in my office in 30 days."

Self-assured, the following day I walked to the unemployment office to find what jobs were available. I did not care that I no longer owned fancy cars to take me anywhere I wanted to go. When I returned home, I began to call businesses and schedule interviews. However, when I revealed that I was an ex-convict on probation, I was quickly dismissed without any further consideration. This happened time and time again. Every day I would get up, and either walk, ride a bike, take a bus, or beg for a ride just to apply for a job. And every day I would get turned down. I was a healthy, young man with a college education, yet I was unable to secure a job. I felt I had no place in society. I was humiliated.

After a year of discouragement and no job, my PO told me I had two more months to find a job or else I would be in violation of my probation. Ultimately, that meant going back to the joint. Being a self-made man who was full of pride, it was hard to ask for help. However,

I had no choice but to swallow my pride if I was going to survive and stay a free man.

I went to a local food bank just to put food on my table, and I had to rely on my grandmother, mother, and my aunt to pay my bills so I could continue to live in my mobile home. Without them, I would not have been able to make it. My feelings of self-worth dropped off the chart as a cloud of depression settled over me. I was anything but happy with my new life. My pride was being broken; my newfound joy in Jesus and my faith were being tested.

I continued my daily efforts to find a job, but rejection dogged my every footstep. At my next scheduled appointment, I told my probation office about my situation. He decided to put me on general relief, which in layman's terms meant I was on welfare. I hit one of the lowest of low points in my life and started to think there was no hope for me to ever be able to support myself. I asked God over and over, "God, where are you?" My faith wavered, and it seemed as though I had traded one chaotic life for another.

When I went to the welfare office to apply for general relief, I was given food stamps and a position working at Bonelli Park in San Dimas, California. The park held special memories for me because, as a kid, I went there with my family to swim and fish. The job was close to home, so I could ride my bike or take a bus and not have to impose on my family.

The job turned out to be a bad joke. Almost everyone who was sent there to work was a drug addict or an alcoholic. Only a few seemed to have a desire to change or find a real job. My duty was to pick up trash, fix sprinkler heads and do whatever else I was told to do. I had no choice. It was either follow orders or go back to jail. Deep down I knew this job was better than nothing, and it was important that I not sit at home and feel sorry for myself.

Yes, my faith was tested, and I felt God had abandoned me, but I refused to let go of the hope I had in Jesus. I knew He was whom He claimed to be, and I held on to the memory of the vision I had while in prison. It was so profound I could not deny it was real. I could not deny that God had miraculously delivered me from my addictions. I could not deny the joy and love I experienced when I asked Jesus to be my Lord and Savior. I held on to the promise that He would never forsake me…ever.

This part of my life lasted for over two years, and I hated every minute of it. As impossible as my situation seemed to be, I was determined to never go back to my previous, sinful lifestyle. I could see the loser I had been reflected in the people who worked around me, and I vowed to never go back and become that person again.

It was during this time of testing that I found out my dad was critically ill. At first, I didn't know how to feel. My thoughts were flooded with memories; my emotions were mixed. I had scarcely had any contact with him for twenty years. I had forgiven my dad for the many ways he had hurt me, but could I love him? I began to think about the many ways I had hurt my Heavenly Father and how He had forgiven me and loved me. How could I not love my dad in the same way God loved me…unconditionally? I could not let Dad die without letting him see the man I had become…without telling him about Jesus.

But I was scared! I had never witnessed to anyone, and I did not have a clue how to even begin. I went to my pastor and asked for help.

With a big grin on his face, Pastor Mark said, "Well, you need to go and fast for a while."

Totally puzzled I asked, "How fast do I need to run?"

My pastor laughed and said, "No, silly…it's not about running; it's about not eating."

Still confused I said, "Not eating? What does that have to do with witnessing?"

He explained, "Jesus tells us that some things are done only through fasting and prayer. That means to go without eating food for a period of time, and at the same time pray and seek God for guidance. That is what you need to do, fast and pray. Then wait and see what God shows you to do."

I did as my pastor suggested and God's Holy Spirit led me to read Psalm 22:3-5 from the Bible. It reads, "Yet you are enthroned as the Holy One; you are the one Israel praises. In you our ancestors put their trust; they trusted, and you delivered them. To you they cried out and were saved; in you, they trusted and were not put to shame." I fasted, and I prayed, and then I went to see my dad.

My nerves were on edge; I was filled with anticipation as I walked into my father's hospital room. I did not have a clue how my visit would go, but I was trusting in Jesus to be there with us. I was unprepared for what I saw when I entered the sterile hospital room. The man I remembered was strong-willed, robust, and full of life…not weak and fragile. This could not be my dad! There were tubes and needles connected everywhere, which caused the man I saw lying there to look even more broken and vulnerable… much like I had been, I thought, when I was in jail.

I stood by Dad's bed for a long time before he opened his eyes and saw me. With difficulty, words stumbled out of my mouth, "D-dad, its m-m-ee. Ron." His eyes lit up in recognition. I can't recall what I said in the next few minutes, but I do recall that it did not take long for me to realize that my father could not speak. His loud, disdainful voice was no more, and I was shocked. Compassion filled me with love as I took my dad's hand in mine. I knew I had to do what I came to do.

After a few minutes of small talk, I calmly said, "Dad we need to have an important conversation. If you are willing to talk to me, squeeze my hand once for yes and twice for no." I felt relief when I felt one weak tug on my hand; he had replied, "Yes."

I started by asking for his forgiveness, "Dad, I have been a rebellious, disrespectful son. I have dishonored and shamed you, and I am so very sorry for all the things that I have done. Please, can you find it in your heart to forgive me?"

He squeezed my hand once again, for yes.

By now tears began to flow down my cheeks. My voice quivered as I instantly felt a change, perhaps healing within me.

"Dad, thank you! Thank you! I can't even begin to tell you how much your forgiveness means to me."

"I want to read something out of the Bible if that is OK."

He squeezed once. I had my dad's attention. He listened intently.

I opened my Bible and read Psalm 22. When I finished reading, I told him the story of Jesus and how He came to offer us forgiveness for our sins and to give us eternal life with Him.

"Dad, I really do love you, and just like Jesus has forgiven me for all the wrong things I have done, I have forgiven you for all the many things you did to hurt me. I don't hate you, and I am no longer angry at you. I want to see you in Heaven where we will live together forever, but first, you have to confess that you are a sinner and ask Jesus to be the Lord of your life. Would you like to do that?"

Without hesitating, he squeezed once. His eyes were beginning to fill with tears.

I was overcome with joy as I continued, "Dad, I am going to pray and each time that I pause that is your time to talk to God in your own words. When you finish talking to God, squeeze my hand, and I will continue. Do you understand?" He squeezed once.

I prayed for a few minutes and then I shared with him the Roman Road to Salvation, a sinner's prayer.[2] In the only way he could, Dad acknowledged that he was a sinner, confessed his past sins, and received Jesus as his Savior. For the first time ever, I saw the love and joy of Jesus, on my father's face. We were both in tears as I found a way around the tubes to hug my father.

He motioned to me with his hands to bring him paper and pencil. He scribbled, "If I get to go home, will you come and read the Bible to me?" I still have that little piece of paper tucked inside the Bible Chaplain Marlin gave me when I was in prison.

I was overcome with emotion and began to openly weep.

"Dad, nothing would bring me more joy than to read God's Word to you every day."

Without a doubt, I knew we would spend eternity together. God had given Dad salvation through Jesus, and as a bonus, He gave me deliverance and healing from all the past hurts centered around my relationship with my father. Jesus also covered my grief and shame over the way I had treated him. I believe Dad was healed from the guilt of the past and how he had treated me. The past was no longer important.

As I left the hospital, I was higher than any drug had ever taken me. Except for my own salvation experience, I had never known such joy. I had witnessed my first salvation miracle, and I was overwhelmed by God's mercy and love.

In the Bible God gave a promise to the Israelites in Joel 2:25, "I will repay you for the years the locusts (grasshoppers) have eaten (your crops)." That day God restored what the powers of darkness had stolen from us. He restored our broken relationship. I went home and cried cleansing tears.

---

2 See the Roman Road to Salvation, a sinner's prayer, at the end of the book.

The following day my dad met Jesus face-to-face. I grieved over the wasted and lost years, but the tears I shed were tears of pure joy because I knew where Dad was. A few days later I had the privilege of speaking at his service and proclaiming his salvation in the Lord Jesus Christ. God used this miracle of grace to show me the path He was leading me to take. My joy and my faith had returned, and I began to understand that God had a unique plan for my life. I still had much to learn.

Not long after my father's passing, I got a new job in a warehouse and eventually became the manager. A year later the business closed down. I quickly found another job delivering batteries. That job only lasted 18 months. At the end of my second year of probation, my PO told me he had observed that I was trying very hard to do what was right. For the next year of probation, I only had to report by mail. When my third year of probation was completed, I was finished. Believe me when I say I was shouting hallelujah. Once again, I was excited about my future.

CHAPTER 13

COMING OUT OF THE WILDERNESS

No words can adequately describe the decade I call my wilderness years. My life had become so different from when I had everything I thought I wanted, or needed, to make me feel I was somebody important. But I was no longer that person because God was teaching me how to be Christ-like. He was slowly peeling away the many layers of my past life that needed to be changed, like pride, impatience, self-centeredness. There were many more layers to be removed, and I knew it would not be easy and would take time. But no matter how long it took, or how many times it took for me to hit rock bottom, I was willing to be completely broken. I told Jesus I was His, and I meant it. My reason for living had changed; I yearned to be used by God to help others.

At the end of my probation in 1993, I called C. Mark Reed, an old friend who had become a Christian. I felt very much alone in the world and desperately needed help. After Mark heard my story, he invited me to attend a men's prayer meeting the following Thursday evening. I agreed to attend the meeting, but when I arrived, I was a nervous wreck.

Pastor Eve introduced me to Mark, Jeff, Joseph, Norman, Johnny, Bill, and Eddie. All the men were friendly, and right away I felt welcomed and accepted.

After introductions and refreshments, each man shared how his week had been. I was relieved when they did not ask me to talk about myself. We read scriptures, and as the prayer time began, the palms of my hands began to sweat, and my heart started to pound. I had prayed very few times privately, but right then I was sure praying that Mark would not call on me. As far as I was concerned praying out loud in front of these men was not going to happen!

When it came to be my turn, I looked wide-eyed at Mark and said, "No way!"

Mark just smiled and said, "Ron, we are your brothers-in-Christ, and we are not here to judge you. We are here to encourage you and to help you. There is no better time than right now to learn how to talk openly to your Heavenly Father." Somehow I sensed it was now or never.

Speaking barely above a whisper, my deep love for praying began, "T-Thank you for g-getting me here, and G-God bless us. Amen."

Mark took me into his life and poured his love for Christ into me. He encouraged the other men to do the same. Each week, for seven years, I faithfully met with them, and for seven years, they faithfully taught me how to be in God's presence and personally with Him through prayer. They taught me how to put my trust in Him. Life continued to be a daily struggle, and if I had not had these men to guide me, I don't think I would have made it through those difficult days.

Not only did these men meet my spiritual needs, they often took care of my physical, emotional and financial needs as well. For many years Norman Blackmer fixed my car free of charge. I cherish the many times we spent together sharing our views on Christianity and politics.

At different times they all fed me and even gave me money when I had none.

Mark and these men hold a special place in my heart, and I will always love them. It has been said that prayer is the key to heaven, but faith unlocks the door. My faith was renewed through the prayers of these men.

Dallas and Betty Beaird also took an interest in me. They went to the same church Mom and I attended. I think they saw something in me I could not see in myself…a future. They became my mentors and taught me about Jesus and how to grow in my relationship with Him. They also showed me how to study the Bible and the importance of having Christian fellowship and prayer.

Dallas wisely wanted me to study three important men in the Bible: Moses, who led Israel out of Egypt—because we both stuttered; David, the shepherd boy who became a king—because of his transparency before the Lord; and Paul, the hater of Jesus who became an apostle—because Dallas saw Paul's likeness in me. I found that I could relate to all three of these ancient men whose stories encouraged me and gave me hope that God could use someone like me to make a difference in this world.

Dallas and Betty treated me with so much dignity, and I often felt like a son to them. Almost weekly, they would graciously slip me a $100 bill to help me pay my bills. They often left large bags of groceries on my doorstep. However, and I say this in jest, there was a price to pay for their kindness. I had to spend time exercising their horses, which I enjoyed. But, shoveling horse manure was another story. So there you have it. I went from drinking champagne to shoveling horse crap. The hard lesson I had to learn was that I had to be willing to start at the bottom with a thankful heart before God could begin to accomplish His purpose in me.

Dallas was very stern with me, as any good ol' Texas boy would be. He taught me the importance of obedience and how to respect and submit to authority. There were times when I wanted to rebel against his discipline of me, but I needed to learn from Dallas what my father did not teach me. Believe me when I say there were times when it was not easy for either one of us. I had a lot to learn. In fact, Dallas also had to teach me about humility, patience, faith, and love. I can still hear his wise words to me, "Ron, have faith in God. Be patient and wait upon Him for the answers. Nothing that matters and lasts will happen in life without faith, patience, and love."

Dallas and Betty had a very successful business, and it was their goal to help me become successful in their business as well. I started working with them, but it did not take long for me to realize I could not give adequate time to a business and to God. I had become dependent on financial security as a drug dealer, and I did not want to be controlled by money again. Yet, the past year without any money at all had been devastating. I was facing one of many crossroads yet to come. I did not know what God's plan was for me, but through the conviction of His Holy Spirit, I knew choosing money and success would be a mistake.

I will be eternally grateful to Dallas and Betty for showing me how to be Jesus to others. They were so kind and patient with me, and I am so thankful for their love and for never giving up on me. I love and respect them so very much and sincerely honor their friendship. I would not have survived without them. Sadly, Betty died in August of 2006; Dallas died just before my book was finished in June of 2018. I miss both of them so very much, but especially Dallas because we frequently kept in touch. My heart aches to think I can no longer pick up the phone and hear his encouraging, affirming words to me.

God brought other life-saving people into my life. My ex-wife, Rhonda, met a woman named Lydia, who was involved in a prison ministry. When Rhonda told her about me and my criminal background, she wanted to get in touch with me. Rhonda asked me to call Lydia, but I said, "Absolutely not!" I did not want to have anything to do with prison… ever again.

Eventually, Rhonda convinced me to call Lydia, and when I finally talked to her, she told me she wanted me to meet her ministry partner, Wally Nelson.

"Why?" I asked Lydia.

"Because I think he would really like to hear your life story," she replied.

Reluctantly, I agreed to call Wally. We made plans to meet at a place called Christ Truth Ministry in Upland, California. After meeting Wally and sharing my story, he asked me to go with him and share my testimony in a prison where he ministered regularly.

"No way!"

I was unrelenting. I would have nothing to do with prisons…ever!

"Will you pray about it?"

I could tell Wally was just as unrelenting as I was.

I promptly bowed my head, closed my eyes and prayed one word, "Amen."

I looked up at Wally and again said, "No w-way!"

Wally's jaw almost dropped to the floor in shock. "You call that a prayer?"

"Yes, that was my prayer."

I turned and walked away without another word. I was done with that conversation. I was done with prisons. And I was done with Wally Nelson.

By the time I got home, I felt rotten and miserable. For some reason, I was mad at Wally. I struggled with my feelings for several weeks, hoping they would go away. They did not.

I ended up calling Wally back and angrily told him, "I don't like you!"

Completely baffled, this gentle, kind, godly man wanted to know why.

"B-because I have to go inside a prison with y-you, and I do not want to. B-but I will ONLY go with y-you just this one time."

Wally was a California Department of Corrections employee and a volunteer chaplain at the California Institution for Women in Chino–Corona, California. He got advanced clearance for me to go inside the prison with him, but when we arrived a few weeks later, entrance was denied because I was not appropriately dressed. Wally, who is usually very calm, did not take the news very well. However, I was delighted.

"S-see, I am n-not meant to go in," I told Wally. "C-can I go home n-now?"

Wally told me to sit down while he went to see the warden about my clearance.

He was grinning, as only Wally could grin, when he returned.

"Let's go! I'm going to buy you some clothes!"

He didn't give me a chance to argue with him, which made me even angrier. Under my breath, I vowed, "This will definitely be my last visit inside any prison."

When we finally got clearance to enter the women's prison, we went into the chapel located in the prison yard where Wally began the church service. He then introduced me to the large group of women inmates. When I stood up and attempted to share my testimony, I was such a nervous wreck I could not control my stuttering. I was totally embarrassed and humiliated. When the meeting was over, I asked Wally to please take me home because I felt like a complete fool.

"Ron, don't you know what happened tonight?" he asked.

Almost in tears, I said, "N-no, I d-don't k-know, and I d-don't care. P-p-please, c-can w-we just l-l-leave?"

Wally looked intently into my eyes and exclaimed, "Ron, because of your testimony half the women here came forward to receive Jesus Christ as their Savior."

Glaring back in disbelief I cried out, "Are y-y-you k-kidding? I s-s-stood there l-like a c-crazy p-person and c-could h-hardly g-get a w-word out of m-my m-mouth."

With great compassion, Wally replied, "They saw your heart Ron…not your deficiency."

That moment changed the direction of my life.

Because of Wally, I was able to identify God's plan for my life. My first experience at witnessing in the prison community changed everything. God was clearly showing me the path He wanted me to take. It was in 1993 that Wally first introduced me to the idea of becoming involved in prison ministry. I found myself at another critical crossroad. It was up to me to choose the road I would take…mine or God's. I had learned that when we become a Christian, we are called to make disciples for Christ. I knew I was being called to make disciples for Jesus through prison ministry. I was also learning I must have faith and trust in God in every area of my life.

Wally became my strongest and wisest mentor. He guided me spiritually for many years and met with me often to disciple, nurture, and spiritually feed me. He was like a father to me, and for that I will be forever grateful.

I was growing in my relationship with Jesus, and I hoped some-day I would be able to make disciples for Jesus who would, in turn, make disciples for Jesus.

CHAPTER 14

FALLING FROM GRACE

My wilderness journey had changed from hopelessness and despair to hope and freedom. The broken pieces of my life were beginning to coming together. As a recent born again Christian, I was taking baby steps toward maturity. There had been many days and nights filled with tears and anguish that were now turning into the pure joy of knowing my Savior, Redeemer, Jesus Christ. The wilderness years were fading into a distant fog as I learned more and more about walking by faith and trusting in God and His Word. Ezekiel 36:26 promises, "I will give you a new heart and put a new spirit in you. I will remove from you your heart of stone and give you a heart of flesh." Jesus was changing the hardness of my heart into a heart of humility.

God used me in many different ways during the early years of my ministry. As mentioned earlier, Wally was the one who first opened the door to new possibilities. Along with a team of volunteers, he got me involved in prison ministry by going into various prisons and jails. Initially, we went to Chino Institution for Women and later Chino Institution for Men. On my own initiative, I went to the California Youth Authority and the Orange County jails with an organization called the

Gleaners. I had the pleasure of meeting and working with Chaplin Ray and Bill Glass Prison Ministries based in Dallas, Texas and personally worked with Chuck Colson and his Prison Fellowship Ministry based out of Washington, D.C. I collaborated with California Rehabilitation Center in Norco, California and Chuckawalla Valley State Prison in Blythe, California. In 1995, I met a man named Harry Lehren during a *Walk to Emmaus* retreat. Through Harry, I became involved with the Kairos Prison Ministry. After becoming involved with Mel Novak's skid row ministry, we became friends. In fact, all these years later, he is one of my most treasured friends. (Later, in 2005, I took Celebrate Recovery, which is a 12-step biblically-based program designed to help those struggling with "hurts, habits, and hang-ups" into prisons with men from Saddleback Church in Lake Forest, California.)

Wally also introduced me to Christ Truth Ministry, which provided a nationwide Bible study correspondence course to prisoners. Upon request, prisoners would receive a Bible lesson from the ministry. A completed lesson would be returned to the ministry where it was graded and then returned to the inmate. I was both surprised and excited when Wally offered me the opportunity to become a grader. Because I had been studying the Bible for several years through a correspondence course offered by Calvary Chapel Church, I felt qualified to accept his offer. I began to spend a few hours every day at Christ Truth Ministry, where I graded lessons and learned the daily, ongoing functions of the ministry.

Steinkamp Prison Ministry also provided a national Bible study correspondence course for prisoners. Wally and Ed Steinkamp were partners and co-founders of both of these non-profit organizations. Ed was a godly, messianic Jewish man who was very successful building homes in Bel Air and Hollywood, California. He was a kind, generous man who gave large amounts of his money to help prisoners through-out the country.

Shortly after Ed's untimely death, his daughter and son-in-law took over the ministry. They quickly realized how difficult it was to run such a large organization and within one year shut it down. Refusing to see this valuable ministry come to an end, Wally asked me to consider taking it over. I felt very confident in my ability to do the job. However, for this to happen an established church would have to become the overseer of the prison ministry.

I had known my pastor in our junior high school days and had been going to his church for about a year. I decided to approach him about the prison ministry's situation. After explaining the circum-stances, I asked him to consider allowing the prison ministry to operate from the church campus. He was very supportive and took my pro-posal to the church elders for consideration. I was overjoyed when I was granted permission to manage the prison ministry from the church, although I would not receive a salary from the church or the ministry. I was told I'd have to depend solely on donations. I was provided a small office from which to work and began my new position as administrator of Steinkamp Prison Ministry with high expectations for my future.

Even though my work for the prison ministry involved super-vising the very important Bible correspondence course within the boundaries of the organized church, I felt my real job was personally working with inmates behind bars where I had once survived *doing time*. Sharing my testimony and making a difference in the lives of these men and women were my passions. This was where I could truly make disciples for Jesus.

Before moving on with my story, I want to speak to the reader who has not yet come to faith in Jesus Christ or who may be a new fol-lower of Christ. By now you may be questioning why you would even want to become, or even continue to be, a Christian. After all, it appears my life has not always been the bed of roses I had expected. The very title of this chapter, *Falling from Grace*, implies that something was about to go down. Well, something did go down, and it was so bad I have a difficult time believing, as a Christian, what I did.

To be honest, I don't want to tell this part of my story, but if I am going to be transparent, I cannot leave it out. On the other hand, I do not want any part of my story to become a stumbling block for anyone who is reading this book. Think back to how many times you have seen me write, "I had a lot learn." Well, keep on counting because Ron Zaucha was a hard nut to crack and still had a lot to learn.

It is important to understand that just because followers of Jesus Christ call themselves Christians, it doesn't mean they always act like Jesus. We are all on a journey that will transform us into the likeness of Jesus Christ. However, our journeys look different because we grow and change at different stages in our Christian walk. Nevertheless, we should never stop seeking God's transforming, healing power.

Some Christians find excuses to continue living in sin, but it is wise to remember that a poor past is a poor excuse for poor behavior. We must all recognize that God's mercy, grace, and forgiveness of our sins do not give us an excuse to continue to sin. We must choose to allow Jesus to change us and the way we behave. Evil behavior brings bondage that brings heartache and suffering; it destroys lives. Godly behavior creates freedom that brings joy and peace.[3]

When I asked Jesus to come into my life I received God's free gift of grace. In other words, even though I did not deserve anything,

---

3 James 3:13-18 teaches us that there are two kinds of wisdom: worldly wisdom and heavenly wisdom. The wisdom of this world should never be mistaken for heavenly wisdom. Worldly wisdom comes from the earthly realm, with the demons. Any place where you find jealousy and selfish ambition, you will discover disorder, confusion, and evil thriving under its rule. But Heavenly wisdom centers on purity, peace, gentleness, mercy, kindness, patience, and love. Righteousness will always be planted in peace by those who embrace Heavenly wisdom.

I was given God's favor—His approval, kindness, and compassion. He forgave every sin I had committed, and He gave me the Holy Spirit to live within me—to guide me, teach me, and help me. Above all else, He gave me the promise of having eternal life in Heaven when I die.

In turn, I gave Him permission to transform me—to change me and work in my life. I wanted to please my Heavenly Father and began to surrender my will—give up my sinful desires and find His will—His perfect desires for me. As my relationship with God through Jesus began to grow...I began to change. I no longer wanted to chase after the evil that I had allowed to controlled me.

Recall that when I received Jesus as my Lord and Savior, I was instantly delivered from my drug and alcohol addiction, and I began to experience peace and love in a new and different way. I also started to think about the interests of others and less about my own self-centered interest. However, I was like an onion being slowly peeled...one layer at a time because there were still kinks in my thinking and my behavior that still need to be worked out. Beneath the surface of my love and faith in Jesus, as I mentioned before, I still carried anger, pride, jealousy, and more in my heart.

Sometimes I still made bad choices but, let me be clear, everyone makes mistakes. No human being will be perfect as long as we live on Earth. However, we are called to do our best to follow Jesus. I had learned the importance of studying the Bible and spending time in prayer. However, I had yet to learn that I was still in danger of making choices that would invite evil demons to influence me. I did not understand that if I listened to Satan's wicked lies he could still tempt me, torment me, and cause me to fall from God's grace.

Since my fall from grace, which I am about to write about, I have learned that Satan can never possess the soul of one who has been born again. I John 4:4 teaches us that He (God) who lives within us is greater than he (Satan) who lives in this world. The Holy Spirit lives within those who are born again.[4] Therefore a demonic spirit cannot live within a Christ follower because of the great power the Holy Spirit of God has over Satan.

However, when we choose to ignore our faith walk with Jesus and step out of the light and protection of God's Holy Spirit, we give Satan permission to influence our minds, our actions, and our lives. When we allow that to happen, we fall from God's grace—we separate ourselves from His divine favor. Since grace is a free gift from our Heavenly Father, we can never fall so far as to lose our salvation, but we can fall far enough away to lose His protection and His blessings. God loved me too much to allow the unhealed wounds of my childhood to continue to influence my bad choices which ultimately caused me to remain the wounded, sinful person I still was.

It has been said that experience is the best teacher. I have found that our experiences will make or break us; they will make us bitter or better. We will either sink or learn to swim because of them. God had to step back and let me fall from grace so that I could learn to swim. He had to let me experience the unthinkable so that I could look at myself through His eyes and admit what I was too blind to see. Otherwise, I would not be able to have a genuine relationship with Him through Jesus.

Keep in mind that my story is about being locked down, and lockdown is not just about being locked behind bars. It is also about being locked down in sin, and even Christians can be locked down in sin. As you continue to read my story, you will see that I was still locked down in areas of my life in which I had not been able to let go. Please

---

4 John 3: 5-7 Jesus answered, "Very truly I tell you, no one can enter the kingdom of God unless they are born of water and the Spirit. Flesh gives birth to flesh, but the Spirit gives birth to spirit. You should not be surprised at my saying, 'You must be born again.'"

keep in mind that ultimately my story is about being set free…finding the path to redemption.

Now back to my story.

I got much satisfaction and pleasure from six incredible years of being involved in various prison ministries. This included managing the Steinkamp Prison Ministry from an office made available to me in the church I attended. This particular ministry flourished under my leadership. I was at peace with my life, and all was going well when I began to date a woman who attended my church.

Marilyn and I fell in love and enjoyed a loving relationship for over a year, but then we began to argue. She had an executive job, made good money, had a beautiful home, and drove a luxury car. All those things I once wanted but no longer had a passion for. I had no real means of support, and since I knew women desire security in a relationship, I felt I had little to offer her. The differences in our financial positions became the underlying fuel that flamed our disagreements.

After a heated argument, I did the unthinkable. I bought a bottle of rum and drank most of it. In fact, I got totally wasted for the first time in over nine years. I got in my car and drove to Marilyn's condo. When I knocked on the door, there was no answer. I could see there were lights on inside so I was convinced she was at home. After pounding on the door several times and still not getting an answer, I peered into her window. I could clearly see two shadows. I was convinced she was with another man.

Sound familiar? Clearly, I did not learn my lesson from the past, and prison must not have been enough to teach me. Satan knew exactly where my weaknesses were…pride, anger, jealousy. He saw my drunken state of mind…defenselessness. He set out to destroy me and my testimony. But God loved me too much to let me stay where I was.

He stepped back and watched *me* derail His perfect plan for my life. And it only took a few minutes to do it.

When I chose to give my body over to alcohol and got drunk, I invited the enemy of my soul back into my life where demonic influences took control of my mind and my actions. I did not realize how dangerous my decision was, especially for me...a professing Christian.

Suddenly I was under the overpowering attack of demonic forces. I was too far gone to turn back. I lost all control of my senses as obsession took over my mind. Blind rage and jealousy led me to return to Marilyn's condo and hunt throughout the parking lot...looking for this other man's car. I didn't know what the man looked like or even if there was another man. I had no idea if he even owned a car or what it looked like. But it didn't matter. I was going to find *his* car. I know this sounds totally crazy, but this is what happened...

The angry, intimidating Ron came to life in the darkness of night. He wandered unwavering in a gorilla-like stance, lingering by every vehicle, attempting to catch the scent of the man in the condo with his woman. Seconds turned into long minutes as he slowly roamed the shadowy parking lot...checking out every possibility. Sniffing! Sniffing! Sniffing like a wild animal searching for his prey! Dark, unseen figures darted around him— prodding him, encouraging him, persuading him. Suddenly, he stopped. Sweat rolling down his face, his eyes glaring, he walked closer. He sniffed—again, and again! Taking one large step forward, he reached out and touched the shiny pickup truck with his clenched fist. He sniffed. He sniffed again. Triumphant, he knew he had his prize! Out of his mind and no longer in possession of his valued guns, he paused— seeking out his next move. He looked in the bed of the truck and spotted a 2x4 piece of wood. Suddenly, he knew! Without hesitation, he grabbed his weapon and began to violently assault the vehicle. Starting at the front of the truck, he methodically destroyed everything he could see with vengeance... the hood, the fenders, the doors. He shattered all of the windows, mirrors, headlights, and tail lights. He left nothing untouched! Exhausted, he threw what was left of the splintered wood into the truck. But the rage had not been satisfied, nor had the old flame burning inside of him, which had suddenly returned, been quenched. He looked at his raw, bleeding hands... unaware... numb. Without warning, emotions surged as he doubled up his fist and slammed it into the battered vehicle...causing further damage...to himself.

It was late the next day when I finally came back to my senses and listened to my voice messages. Marilyn knew precisely who was guilty of such a violent act against, not just her friend, but against her. After telling me what she thought of me, she threatened to tell the church what I had done. Still hung over, the reality of what I had done began to sink in as the voice message abruptly ended.

Regret slowly turned into dread as conviction turned into fear. In my mind, I was convinced she was having an affair, but I knew that did not justify my actions.

What had I done? What was I going to do?

In a daze, I called a trustworthy friend, Eric. I told him what had happened to an acquaintance of mine the night before and that I wanted to get his opinion about what the guy should do. Right away Eric knew I was lying and that I was talking about myself. When he confronted me, I had to admit that I was the guilty one. Eric advised me to immediately contact my pastor.

By the time I made the call to my pastor, Marilyn had already given him her account of the dreadful situation. I was distraught as I tried to tell my side of the story. He listened patiently and then thanked me for being man enough to come to him directly and own up to what I had done. He my told me if I wanted to continue in the ministry I would have to get counseling from the church's executive pastor, and I would be put on probation.

I was beside myself with worry, but diligent to do everything I was asked to do. But it made no difference. Meetings were held without my knowledge. Trust was broken on all sides, and the entire incident came with devastating consequences. You cannot go back and change the past or change what people think about you. Eventually, I lost my fiancé and my ministry position. Everything I had worked so hard for was gone, and I did not know where I was going or what I was going to do. I left feeling vulnerable, disillusioned, and angry.

The Bible tells us that Satan roams the world seeking whom he can overcome.[5] The night I consumed the bottle of rum, the powers of darkness were watching as I gave Satan the opportunity, once again, to get a hold on me and set me up to be a failure. Worst of all, this time I failed as a born-again believer in Jesus Christ. In timely fashion, he even dropped a golden nugget right in front of me, which I snatched up without a moment's hesitation.

Rick, my old friend from Maui, called with the job offer of a lifetime. I was on a plane to Hawaii faster than a bullet flying out of the Smith & Wesson I once owned.

The golden nugget turned out to be the perfect dream job I had hoped for during my drug dealing days. It had incredible perks which included housing, a car, travel expenses and an over-the-top salary. I would be traveling the world filming rock concerts.

As soon as I got off the plane in Maui, Rick told me Dave Mason, a popular rock star, had a concert scheduled for the following night. Rick was in charge of filming the concert and was thrilled about me being there to work with him. We spent the next day getting everything

---

5 I Peter 5:8 "Be alert and of sober mind. Your enemy the devil prowls around like a roaring lion looking for someone to devour."

set up. Before the concert started, Rick gave me a VIP badge that gave me access to all venues connected to the event. I roamed around backstage for a while and eventually wandered into what is known as the "green room" where only celebrities and their guest are allowed.

The moment I opened the door and stepped inside I felt the haunting, familiar oppression. My past demons, booze, and cocaine confronted me. There was an abundant supply of beautiful, sexy women everywhere I looked. A disgusting feeling began to churn within me as my eyes scanned the large room and saw half-naked women exposing their bodies in a way that at one time would have turned me on. But instead, I felt sick as I stood and watched.

Without warning, I felt someone grab my butt. Startled, I looked around to find a voluptuous blonde standing behind me. Her sultry voice whispered in my ear, "Do you want to go over in the corner and get…"NO!" I yelled, not letting her finish. Every nerve in my body began pulling my senses in different directions as voices inside my head simultaneously tormented me.

"Yes, stay!" "No, run!"

"Choose temptation!" "No, choose freedom!"

"Do you really want to be free?" "The truth will set you free!!"

Finding my voice, I shouted at the stunned woman, "I've g-got to g-get out of h-here."

I darted out of the "green room" and rushed back to the concert arena. The rock music I once loved sounded loud and offensive; my head began to throb. I frantically searched for an empty chair. My legs felt weak, and I feared they would buckle beneath me.

I found a place to sit down and buried my face in my shaking hands. No one could hear me moan, "What am I doing here? Why did I ever come to this place?"

I could not trust myself to mingle backstage, so I remained in my seat until Rick found me after the concert. When he called out to me I could tell he was stoned. "Let's go, Bro. It's time to party!"

I told him I did not want to go to the after-party. Not persuaded, he grabbed my arm and led me outside. I can't explain why, but I climbed into Rick's car, and we head for Wailea, Maui.

Once at the party, I roamed throughout the spacious house with all its lavish decorations. I had taken pleasure in these parties for twenty years, but this time I was looking through very different lenses. I saw the alluring women; I knew they were not so glamorous on the inside. I heard the giddy laughter; I knew it was fake. I saw the drugs and alcohol; they represented evil and death. I witnessed the lust of the flesh openly displayed; I knew it was sin. A wave of nausea washed over me.

There are times in life when you are faced with problems that only you and you alone have the ability to solve. This was one of those times, and I knew there would be no second chance if I chose to stay. I had spent the last ten years learning that life is about choices and about consequences. I had already suffered the outcome of too many bad decisions, and I did not want to go there again. I thought about my recent fall from God's grace that had led me back to this place, and I knew this moment was more than a crossroad. It was not just a place where I could choose to go down one path or another. It was a crucial point in my life where I had to make a decision. This had to be the finale, the end for me. I knew that I could never, nor would I ever, be that same old Ron Zaucha again.

It was not an audible voice that I heard, but a still small voice within me, "Your past no longer has power over you unless you let it have power. You have to deny that power and take control over it once and for all."

I found Rick, and told him I had to go home.

He said, "Just take my car, and I will see you back at my place later."

"No Rick! You don't understand. I can't g-go b-back to this life. I am going home to California w-where I belong."

"Ron, are you crazy? This is the dream job we always wanted! Just you and me! Bro, I want you here with me!"

Unmoved, I made it very clear to my friend that I was done.

"If I stay here, I'll return to a way of life that I no longer want and or have the guts for. And I will die."

Waving my hand around the room, I continued, "I don't want to have anything to do with all of this."

Rick was visibly stunned by my response, but I didn't care. I was fighting for my very survival…something he could not possibly understand at the time. I caught the next available plane out of Maui and never looked back.

My fall from grace was exactly what I needed to open my eyes. I had to take a hard look at myself and turn to God's Word to find the answers. In the Bible, the Lord declared in Isaiah 66:2, "These are the ones I look on with favor: those who are humble and contrite (broken, sorry, remorseful, ashamed) in spirit, and who tremble at my word." I wanted my life to be a sign of God's favor toward me.

Romans 12:2 guided me. "Do not be conformed to this world, but be transformed by the renewing of your mind." I had to allow God's Holy Spirit to change my thinking which was done by *believing* that His promises in the Bible were for me. I had to sincerely desire to change my old habits and bad behavior. Only then would I begin to understand what it truly meant to be Christ-like in my behavior.

CHAPTER 15

GOD IS GREATER THAN ANY PROBLEM

When I returned to California after leaving Hawaii, my future was uncertain. I thought I was finished. I felt rejected and hurt by my church. In fact, I thought I was through with Christian ministry. But God had other plans, and He loved me too much to leave me with unfinished business. It was time for another lesson, or two. Clearly, I had not learned my lesson the first time I lost control and used a shot gun to shoot up a vehicle and, went to prison! The Bible guided me as I began to discover the healing power of forgiveness.

In fact, Jesus taught a lot about giving and receiving forgiveness. Even as he hung on the cross, he pleaded with His Father, "Forgive them for they know not what they are doing." Luke23:34

He taught us to pray in Matthew 6:12 (KJV), "Forgive us our debts as we forgive our debtors."

And Matthew 6:14 and 15 tells us that if we forgive those who sin against us the Father will forgive us. But if we do not forgive others, the Father will not forgive us.

In Matthew 18:22, Peter, the disciple, asked Jesus how often was it necessary to forgive and Jesus replied, "Seventy-seven times."

In other words, as often as you have to, you must forgive. It is the key that unlocks many doors that lead to healing of mind, body, soul, and relationships.

I could not stay bitter and angry. I had to forgive the church and the prison ministry board for the unjust way I felt I was treated and seek forgiveness from God for letting my pride and jealousy, once again, turn to booze, rage, and destruction. And I had to seek forgiveness from Marilyn and her friend for turning my rage onto them. And finally, I had to accept after all was said and done that I was responsible for getting myself into the mess I was in. I had to forgive myself and walk in mercy for others because that is what Jesus had done for me. I prayed others would show mercy and forgive me also.

The bottom line is this: If Jesus can forgive me for all that I have done, how can I possibly withhold forgiveness from anyone?

Had I not personally experienced who Jesus is, I would have walked out of the Christian-based community and never gone back. But once again God had godly men waiting in line to help me make the transition back to His will for my life. Mel Novak, the Skid Row minister I mentioned earlier, was one of those men.

Mel stood by me when I was dismissed from the church prison ministry. Even though Wally Nelson had planted the seeds years before, it was Mel who encouraged me to get my own prison ministry up and running. In fact, he was the catalyst God used to start Lighthouse Educational Ministries. When I reminded Mel I had no money to start a ministry, he told me to pray about it. Consequently, Mel and a host of other men, who had taken an interest in me, provided the funds I needed.

At the same time all of this was going on, Kevin, whom I had ministered to while he was an inmate in Chino, was released from prison. He called and asked what I was up to. When I told him I had been given an opportunity to get my own ministry started, Kevin told me he could help me out. He knew all about setting up a nonprofit status organization and immediately began to get all of the necessary paperwork in order. Once nonprofit status was established, Lighthouse Educational Ministries Inc. was founded in February 2001.

Before I left for Maui to work with Rick, Pastor Chuck Singleton, my friend and senior pastor of Loveland Church in Fontana California told me, "You will not take the job, and you will be back." I strongly suspect that Pastor Chuck and his congregation were on their knees, in spiritual warfare, praying for me.[6] After returning from Maui, Pastor Chuck offered me a job as his associate pastor. I accepted the position as Pastor of Evangelism and Prison Ministry. My role was to develop materials for evangelism and also organized outreach events in the community.

At my pastor's suggestion, I made plans to move closer to the church. My precious mother came to Fontana to go house shopping with me. When she saw this one particular residence, she declared, "Ron this is the perfect place for you." I trusted her judgment, and with the financial help from my cousin, David, I bought my first house in Fontana, California. My mom is now in Heaven with Jesus, and I often find myself wishing she was still around to give me advice and encouragement.

Being one of the few white faces in Pastor Chuck's congregation was a bit awkward at first. However, all the church members made me feel very welcome and comfortable. Not only did they love and

---

6 "For our struggle is not against flesh and blood, but against the rulers, against the authorities, against the powers of this dark world and against the spiritual forces of evil in the heavenly realms." Ephesians 6:10

accept me, but they were also very generous to me financially. My time there was invaluable because I learned so much under Pastor Chuck's Biblical teachings. It was at Loveland Church where I experienced what true worship is about and where I witnessed the work and power of the Holy Spirit. No high on drugs can compare to the high I got from worshiping with my new church family. It was there God set me free from the prejudices of my childhood...among other things. An extra bonus was being there when entertainers Smokey Robinson and Natalie Cole often came to sing for us.

I enrolled in a seminary school called Vision International University in Ramona, California, which gave me the opportunity to do in-depth studies of the Bible. God proved faithful to His Word. As I spent hours pouring myself into the scriptures, I continued to be "transformed by the renewing of my mind."[7] I received my bachelor's degree in theology in 2001 graduating with a 3.75 GPA, which was a miracle for someone who was once a long-time, hardcore drug addict.

During the time I was a pastor at Loveland Church, I got involved with Celebrate Recovery at Saddleback Church in Lake Forest, California. I continued to go into prisons to teach the message of Jesus, and I trained others how to do prison ministry.

After living in Fontana for about two years, I took a second loan on my house and bought an apartment. A year later I sold both for a substantial profit and moved to nearby Hesperia, California, where I was able to purchase five houses, one of which I lived in. Seeing another investment opportunity, I sold my home in Hesperia, and with the profit gained I was able to buy a house Coto De Caza, California.

In 2005, while still working for Pastor Chuck, I felt led to turn my four remaining homes in Hesperia into halfway houses as part

---

7 Romans 12:2 "Do not conform to the pattern of this world, but be transformed by the renewing of your mind. Then you will be able to test and approve what God's will is...his good, pleasing and perfect will."

of my own prison ministry. I received many financial promises from Christians and Christian organizations to help keep them open, but few of those promises materialized. Consequently, I spent four years managing these houses with my own funds.

When a Christian counselor pledged to keep the houses filled if they were licensed, my mother—whose financial means were meager—donated a substantial amount of money to the ministry to pay for the license fees. The counselor did not keep her word. Consequently, I continued to struggle with keeping the halfway houses open while operating Lighthouse Educational Ministry, and working for Pastor Chuck.

In 2007, a decision was made to leave Loveland Church. I wanted to devote all my time to my own prison ministry. It was hard to leave Pastor Chuck and the wonderful people who had faithfully loved and supported me.

In February 2008, a significant stock market crash hit America which negatively impacted the housing market. The halfway houses had to be refinanced just to keep them open. I went $100,000 in debt trying to keep from losing my properties and my ministry. It was recommended I consider bankruptcy protection, which I refused to do because I did not think it would be honoring to God. I walked away from four of my houses, and with the help of a debt consolidation company, I eventually paid off my debt. My decision left me with a ruined credit rating, and all that I had worked so hard for the ministry was gone. It was evident that if something didn't change I would soon be homeless. I did not have a clue what was going to happen.

My stress level was off the charts. In August 2008, I passed out at the gym because of an undiagnosed genetic defective aortic valve. I had been a walking dead man all of my life and didn't know it. My heart could no longer take the stresses I demanded of it. Open heart surgery was immediately scheduled.

While in the hospital, a man I had recently met visited me and graciously invited me to recover at his house. I stayed with Albert (not his real name) for a month before returning to my one remaining house in Coto De Caza.

All of the financial issues I was dealing with were going on while I was trying to recover from major surgery. But in spite of everything, I continued to trust in Jesus, and he faithfully carried me through those difficult times. I could not help but question why God had allowed all of this to happen. I did not understand, but I knew there were still lessons for me to learn. I sincerely wanted Him to show me what He was trying to teach me.

Two months after returning to my home, Albert called and offered me a job with his company. I saw his offer as a way to help me get on my feet financially so that I could get my prison ministry back on track, save my house, and have a way to support myself. In my mind, I felt these were all logical reasons to take the job. So, I packed up, moved, and began a career in an industry I knew nothing about. I honestly don't think I was trusting God when I made this decision. Given the situation I was in, as I said before, it seemed a logical thing to do so I just did it. It would be one of the worst decisions of my life.

The circumstances that followed are too long and confusing to write about in detail so I will make this part of my story as short as possible.

I fell in love with the idea behind the Christian-based business I went to work for. I saw it as a way to lead young people into a personal relationship with Jesus. I was given specific responsibilities which I performed with confidence.

I had no reason to have any knowledge about the financial/business side of the company. After a while, Albert started to share different ideas with me about how to fund the distribution of his product. He decided it would be a good idea for me to form a separate company. So, when Albert told me what he wanted me to do and offered me a sizeable increase in salary, I was sold on his plan. I had no reason to question his judgment or his word.

His lawyers prepared all of the necessary, legal documents. I naively signed them without fully understanding what I was getting into. I gave Albert absolute authority and full discretionary power over the company, which was set up in my name. After all, I was a licensed, ordained minister and had been operating a non-profit prison ministry for eight years. I had no experience as a CEO or managing a corporation.

About a year later, Albert told me the two companies would be going through an audit, and all business would stop until some issues were resolved. Beyond that, I was not given any additional information. Shortly thereafter, because of the business arrangement Albert had devised for me, I was served as a co-defendant in a case against Albert by the Securities and Exchange Commission. My biggest nightmare began as I found myself in an unbelievable situation.

The entire incident is so complicated that to this day I still don't understand why I was charged with anything at all other than guilty by association. I was not an attorney who was familiar with the business law, and I did not have experience regarding stocks, nor did I know how the SEC worked. If you recall, after a judge sent me to prison for evaluation, a prison counselor called me stupid. Well...that also applied in this situation. I naively signed papers I did not understand and trusted the wrong people.

A judgment was placed against me by the presiding judge. Based upon my lawyer's advice, I gave up and accepted the judge's ruling because I did not have the hundreds of thousands of dollars needed to continue defending myself. I was also terrified to think I might be sent back to prison if I did not accept the ruling.

However, the worst thing about accepting the judgement was that I didn't realize my ministry supporters, and people in general, would perceive this acceptance as an admission of guilt. My reputation was tarnished, and people judged me without knowing all the facts; I was seen to be the hardened criminal I once was. But I know that I was not then, nor am I now that person. Most important of all, God knows I am innocent of any wrongdoing when it comes to the SEC case against Albert.

I did not set out to get rich when I bought the properties which I used as halfway houses for prisoners. My intentions were good. But in hindsight, I can see that perhaps subconsciously there was still a part of me that identified self-worth with owning "things." God was showing me that I didn't need to own those houses and that I just needed to trust in Him to provide.

Likewise, I did not set out to get rich when I went to work for Albert. I just wanted to support my prison ministry and myself. Again, my intentions were good, but I was looking for a "worldly" way to reclaim what I had lost and to provide for my future. Once again, God was showing me I did not need to go out and make a lot of money, but I needed to depend entirely on Him for all my needs, and that meant depending on Him for everything.

I must admit there were times when it was difficult to wrap my mind around the "why" questions. But now...I clearly understand that God was answering my prayers when I asked Him to show me what He was trying to teach me. Proverbs 3:5-6 declares, "Trust in the Lord with all your heart. Lean not unto your own understanding. Acknowledge him in all you ways and He will direct your path." All He wanted me to do was trust Him, and it has been through my failures that I have learned I *can* trust Him. I've learned from God's Word—the Bible—there is a better way than my way.

In Matthew 19:16-30 there is a story about a rich man who approached Jesus and asked what he had to do to get to heaven. In verse 21 Jesus replied, "If you want to be perfect, go, sell your possessions and give to the poor, and you will have treasures in heaven. Then come, follow me."

The key to this verse for me is…"*then* come, follow me." God does not ask everyone to go sell their possessions, and I don't think he cares if people are wealthy as long as their wealth does not become a stumbling block or a hindrance to having a relationship with Jesus. But for those of us who have been called into a missionary type of ministry, His expectations are different. As long as we are tied to money and possession, we will not fully and completely go and follow Him.

I Timothy 6:5-10 tell us, "People think godliness is a means to financial gain, but godliness with contentment is a great gain. We brought nothing into the world, and we can take nothing out of it. But if we have food and clothing, we will be content with that. Those who want to get rich fall into temptation and a trap, and into many foolish, and harmful desires that plunge people into ruin and destruction."

The key to his scripture for me is…"we will be content." I must learn to be content with what I have so that I won't fall into a foolish trap.

I Timothy 6:10 warns us, "For the love of money is a root of all evil. Some people, eager for money, have wandered from the faith and pierced themselves with much grief."

The key to this scripture for me is…"some have wandered from the faith and pierced themselves with much grief." God knew my history. He knew my previous love for money and that the job with Albert had the potential for pulling me away from ministry and away from

His will for me. Never forget that Satan knows our weaknesses and He will try to pull us toward them. I went after the salary, with good intentions, instead of trusting in God to provide the way—His perfect way. He loved me too much to leave me in a place outside of His perfect plan for my life.

Ephesians 4:22 taught me that "Regarding my former way of life, I am to put off my *old self* which is being corrupted by its deceitful desires."

It is my prayer that I will never forget what God has shown me about myself. I never want to hurt Him so deeply again.

It has been seven long years since the SEC judgment was made against me. When that happened, I fell harder than I ever thought I could fall. My faith was stretched. My ministry suffered. I was called a crook. I was rejected and misunderstood. I felt as though I had been stripped naked. I was broken. But then, isn't that what happened to Jesus? Isn't that what he had to endure for all of humanity...for me, for you?

I am in no way comparing my suffering to the suffering of Jesus, but He knew there were still broken, ragged pieces in my life that had to be repaired and put back together. Only God knew what it would take to make that happen. Most often, it is in our suffering and pain that we find God and learn to trust in Him completely.

I Thessalonians 5:18 reminds us to, "Give thanks *in* all circumstances, for this is God's will for you in Christ." We are not being told to thank God *for* what happens to us, but we are being told to give thanks because we have an opportunity to put our trust in God, believing He will bring mercy and grace into the events of our lives.

My faith and trust in God are stronger than ever before. It took me a long time to learn that I could praise and thank Him *in* all situations, no matter what the outcome might be because this *is* His will for me. When I fully accepted that God is greater than any problem I have, everything in my life changed.

I often lean on the words of Corrie Ten Boom, a Dutch lady who hid Jews from the Nazis in World War II, "You can trust your *unknown* future to a *known* God."

As of this writing, in 2018, negotiations for settling with the SEC began. Results are pending, but I know that my God is working to use this situation for my good, to His glory, and to finally bring closure to this chapter of my life.

CHAPTER 16

WHY I DO WHAT I DO

Harper Lee wrote in her famous book *To Kill a Mockingbird*, "You never really know a man until you understand things from his point of view...until you climb into his skin and walk around in it."

I am often asked, "Why do you go back to prisons and do what you do? What's the point?" Some have commented that there is no money to be gained by what I do, and I should get a regular job and do ministry part time so I can pay my bills. My response is that prison ministry deserves my full attention—not just part of my attention. I do admit there are times when it is difficult to keep going. True, there is no financial value in what I do, and there are times when I wonder how I will make it through another day, month or year. And there are times when I get discouraged and start to think that no one really cares. But then...when I go into a prison, and climb into the skin of someone who is only surviving there, everything changes because I remember the young man I once was.

Not only do I understand what it is like to be locked behind bars, I identify with the dysfunction and bad choices that got the men and women there in the first place. Like Jesus walked in the shoes of humanity, I have walked in the shoes of those incarcerated. Our stories may be different, but parts of our journeys remain the same. I want inmates to know they have hope once they return to the real world, and I give them hope when I tell them about Jesus. I have been called by God to be in prison ministry for a reason. Considering the number of prisons and prison inmates in the United States, besides a few brave souls like me, there does not appear to be near enough people who are taking up the charge to minister to prisoners.

Following are just a few stories which will help explain why I do what I do. (You will find additional stories in the "Testimonials" toward the back of this book.)

When my mother and my ex-wife, Rhonda, visited me on Sunday, they would purchase a carton of cigarettes from the vending machine and give them to me. This was back when smoking was allowed inside prison walls. Since I did not smoke, I used them to barter for food and clothing. Instead of dealing drugs, I was dealing cigarettes. This was after I had my vision of Jesus but had not yet been convicted of all of my bad habits. I met many men who had been sentenced and were serving third and fourth terms. One of those men, Gary, was in for a long stretch and had no money. I decided to use my "bartering funds" to help him get some of the things he needed.

"What do you want in return?" he questioned.

"I want nothing."

He responded with mistrust. "Nothing is free in the Joint."

I explained, "Gary, I am going to leave this place soon, but you are going to be stuck here for a long time. When men come in here and have needs, you can pay it forward. In other words, you can do for them what I have done for you."

"Zaucha, you are a strange duck."

Ignoring his comment I continued, "I'm a Christian, and I'm just trying to do what is right."

Gary was a big guy, full of tattoos. "Well, if anyone messes with you tell me, and I will handle them."

"Thank you, but I have someone bigger than you protecting me."

Confused, the man looked around and said, "Where is he? I don't see anyone lookin' out for you."

I told him, "It is Jesus. He is always with me…and He is with you too. All you have to do is believe in Him."

He thought for a few seconds and then mumbled, "Maybe someday I will."

I wrote to Gary for three years after I was released. Finally, I got the letter I had been waiting for. "Ron, I am a Christian now because of you. I watched many men in prison professing to believe in Jesus, but none of them ever did for me what you did."

One of the most haunting places I have ever been invited to share my testimony is Skid Row, which is roughly a 50-block area in downtown Los Angeles. This locale is home to the largest concentration of homeless people in the country where streets are lined with makeshift dwellings of cardboard, plywood, and plastic tarps.

My buddy, Mel Novak, whom I have mentioned earlier, has ministered on Skid Row for over 30 years. He invited me to share my testimony with men and women of all ages who were dirty, smelly, wore ragged clothing, slept on sidewalks, and dug around in trash cans for food. I was taken aback by the hopelessness I saw in the eyes of what appeared to be numb, empty shells walking around with a mindset that no one cared about them…that their lives did not matter. Their only purpose in life seemed to be surviving another day.

This turned out to be one of the most humbling experiences in my life because I quickly realized that this could be me. I saw people living on the streets that I had also seen in prison. One day a woman walked up to me and said, "Do you remember me? I was in Chino Prison."

I remember thinking…and now you are homeless?

After my first visit on Skid Row, I went home and thanked God that I had a roof over my head, a bed to sleep in, hot water to bathe in and food on my table. And most important of all, I had no fear of being harmed. I thanked God for my mother and grandmother, who prayed for me, never gave up on me, and helped me financially when I had no money and could not get a job. I thanked God for the men and women He put in my life along the way to mentor and to teach me the difference between making good and bad choices. I wouldn't have made it without them.

I gave much thought to the question, "What if I had not had these people in my life?" The answer was simple. I would be homeless, without hope, surviving…not living. It is even probable that I would be in jail for life or dead.

I began to understand why many of the homeless go back to prison. At least in prison, the homeless have a feeling of belonging somewhere. And even if it's not always safe in prison, it's safer than the streets, and they have a warm place to sleep and something to put in their stomach.

I am thankful that Mel still leaves the door open for me to minister on Skid Row as often as I can. It is my heart's desire to tell prisoners and ex-prisoners what Jesus did for me…to give hope to the hopeless.

Very early in my ministry, I went with Wally to the men's prison in Chino where I had been incarcerated. Ironically, I shared the Gospel message in the same chapel where I had heard it years before. I set the stage for my message by asking an inmate to stand up and let me sit in his chair. I then related my own personal experience to the men who had come to hear me speak.

"I once sat in this exact same spot. Now it is a privilege for me to come back and tell you my story and to share God's Word. I understand why some of you get set free but most often find yourself back in prison. It's tough to return to a society that doesn't seem to have a place for you. But I'm here to tell you that you don't have to come back to this place. There is a better way of life for each one of you. I never want to return, and I never will because I found true freedom in having a relationship with God through Jesus. I want to tell you how to meet Jesus and how to be set free from the sins in your life that sent you here. I never want you to come back either, except to do what I'm doing now."

Recently, I saw the 2017 feature documentary, *Steve McQueen: American Icon*. As a youth, the late actor spent time in the Boys Republic, a reformatory in Chino Hills, California. As an adult, he devoted time to the institution, a private, nonprofit, school and treatment community for troubled youngsters. Since its founding in 1907, it has guided more than 30,000 at-risk teenage boys and girls toward productive, fulfilling lives.

As I watched the movie about Steve McQueen's life, I realized how much I had in common with the performer. Like McQueen I have a sincere desire to reach out to troubled youths who are where we both were years ago. I decided to make arrangements to visit the Boys Republic facility. When I left the detention center on the day of my visit, I felt a renewed commitment to help young people find a way out of the darkness and despair that had put them there... before they ended up like me and in prison.

Before moving away from the subject of the youth of today, I want to share my personal thoughts concerning young people and their families.

A decaying culture will always set youngsters up for failure. I did not think it could get as bad as it was when I was a kid but, in fact, it is much worse. More than ever before our kids need help. They are all susceptible to evil's snares, and it does not matter if they are rich or poor. They all need to understand that consequences always follow the choices they make, and ultimately only they can determine the outcome.

Many young people, who have ended up in trouble with the law, come from "privileged" homes and often have parents who work outside the home to pay for the privileges their children enjoy. Therefore, many of these kids come home from school to empty houses. They have unsupervised time on their hands, unlimited access to the internet and money in their pockets to spend. They are vulnerable and subject to peer pressures.

They seldom have conversations with their parents about what is going on in their lives and are given little or no moral guidelines. When parents get home at the end of a long day, they often consume alcohol (or maybe even drugs) to help them cope with their stress. Kids are like sheep and will follow in their parents' footsteps by finding their own way to deal with their struggles. They start to use alcohol, which leads to the use of drugs and becoming sexually active. These behaviors can result in addictions, deadly accidents, diseases, unwanted pregnancies, suicides and destroyed lives. Because there is no authority figure in the home, rebellion against life, in general, can take control often with devastating consequences.

For most children who come from "underprivileged" homes, I can paint the same picture to describe their home lives. The basic difference is the lack of money, material possessions, and a welfare system that keeps the poor dependent. These kids want what they do not have. The consequences are often the same except these young people frequently become involved in criminal activity to acquire what the "privileged" have or just to provide for the basic needs in life.

My past experience in counseling with young people has taught me they are generally afraid to get real and say what they need to say. However, their responses to me usually change when I say, "Let me tell you about me." Most youths are wiser than we give them credit for and will listen to what you have to say if they feel you're sincere…if you are real with them.

Those who will speak up usually express the same kinds of frustration. "My parents don't love me. They don't spend time with me. They don't discipline me. If they really loved me, they would correct me, but they don't. They don't care what I do." All these kids want is to know they are loved by their parents. They just want to know they matter, and that someone cares about them.

Ministering especially to underprivileged kids breaks my heart because I see myself in them. I want to fix them, but I can't. I can only try to help them understand that drugs, sex, and money did not bring me happiness. In fact, those *things* stole my dignity, self-respect, self-esteem, pride, joy, my ability to receive love and to give love, and ultimately they stole many years of my life—and they landed me in prison. All of this happened because I made horrific, bad choices. However, by God's grace those good qualities were given back to me, and more. One of the most important things I can say to the youth of today is to please understand that *you* have the power to choose the life *you* will have.

The youth of today must also understand how important it is to pick their friends wisely because those "friends" will have an effect on their future and their lives. If they want to be a criminal, then hang out with criminals. If they're going to be successful, then hang out with people who have goals and a future.

Kids need to realize why it is important to respect authority, including their parents, and why getting an education is so important. Visiting a school counselor and asking for help in planning a career path can be invaluable to their future.

If parents don't provide a stable environment at home, kids can go to the local YMCA or a church and ask for a mentor...someone who will invest time in them.

Above all else, young people should pay close attention to these words: Do not decide that your fate to be a failure has already been determined. You have the power to choose to be a good, law-abiding citizen or to be a criminal. You can decide to live in a jail cell or to live in freedom. You can change the direction your life is going if it is not what you want it to be.

I feel it is important for me to address parents and their responsibility to their children. Being a parent is the most difficult job in the world, and they need all the help they can get. No one gets it right all of the time. However, I have a few things I would like to communicate to parents before continuing with my story.

First and foremost, don't try to be your child's friend. They need you to be their parent from the moment they take their first breath. Take parental responsibility and don't stray from what is right, no matter how hard it may be.

Don't give them everything they want and do not be afraid of them.

Teach them responsibility and discipline as soon as they take their first steps. It seldom works if you suddenly turn into a caring, involved parent when your kids become teenagers.

Habits, good and bad, are formed early in life. Begin giving children chores around the house when they are very young so that, when they are older, doing chores will not become an issue. As they mature, encourage them to find a responsible job.

Don't wait until children are teens to set up clear boundaries. Communicate rules to them when they are toddlers. Let them know immediately when they cross forbidden lines. Kids will rebel and test parents because they really want to know there is a line they cannot cross.

When children disobey, discipline them. It will not be easy but don't ever give in to them. When rules are reinforced over and over, kids will understand and know they are loved.

When I was younger, my mother found marijuana in my room and put it in the trash. When I discovered it missing, I defiantly told her she had better go get it because I owed someone money for it. I told her I was going to leave the house, and when I got back, it had better be where she found it. She put it back without saying a word to me.

This is a perfect example of a parent who was afraid to be a parent and hesitant to accept parental authority over her child who was making bad choices. She should have told me to be quiet and remind me that I was living in her house, and as long as I lived there, I would follow her rules. If I didn't like her rules, I could move out.

I was the perfect example of a rebellious, disrespectful, out of control kid who made many bad choices and ended up in prison. I fully accept responsibility for my actions and do not blame my mother for anything that happened to me.

The bottom line is this: our society has bought into the "keeping up with the Joneses" lie. It really does not matter what the bank account looks like. What our kids really want is parents who care enough about them to help them grow up to be responsible, good people. The big house and fancy cars cannot replace time spent with them. Things cannot replace love. If you want to keep your kids out of prison, you must start a relationship with them the day they are born. Talk to them, communicate with them, and get to know them.

It is never too late to find out how your children define love. Above all else, find out who their friends are because peers will have more influence over them than you do. If you are emotionally absent from their lives, if you don't act like the parent, your children will find ways to fill the void they feel by your absence.

By now, it should go without saying…the most crucial thing is to tell them about Jesus.

So why do I do what I do? The answer is simple. I go back into the prison system because "There but for the grace of God go I."[8] After experiencing firsthand what prisoners go through and knowing how little help they receive while doing time or after being released, how can I not go back and minister to those who remain? I desire to reach out to as many as possible. I want to give them insights that I did not have before I began my journey to freedom.

I return time and time again because of all the "Gary's" who have made bad choices but are willing to make the right decisions by accept Jesus as their Lord and Savior.

I return for those who have problems with substance abuse and who are impacted by the criminal justice system.

Life has trained me and equipped me to be an encouragement and inspiration to all inmates, and this is what I want them to tell them:

There were many times when I could have killed someone or been killed, and many times when my bad choices could have utterly destroyed me. I am convinced that even though I did not see God, He was always with me...watching over me...just like he is watching over you now.

Inmates are often forgotten within the system and have no one outside prison walls who care about them. Having said that, I want prisoners to realize that just because they do not have outside help, or they do not have someone praying for them, God is always present.

Psalm 139:1-7 tells us that God is all knowing and all present.

Oh Lord, you have searched me, and you know me.
You know when I sit down and when I arise.
You perceive my thoughts from afar.

---

8   Allegedly from a mid-sixteenth-century English evangelical preacher and martyr, John Bradford, "There but for the grace of God go I." This was in reference to a group of prisoners being led to execution.

You discern my going out and my lying down;
You are familiar with all my ways.
You hem me in from behind and before;
You have laid your hand upon me.
Such knowledge is too wonderful for me,
Too lofty for me to obtain.
Where can I go from your Spirit?
Where can I flee from your presence?

No one can escape the presence of our Holy God. We are all His children, and He waits patiently for His children to seek Him. He is only a prayer away, and His son, Jesus, will be their friend if they will only invite Him into their lives.

Prison ministry gives me the opportunity to be Jesus to inmates… to be someone who cares, and to point the way for them to find Jesus. If I was important enough for Jesus to save me, then I must show others they are just as important to Him.

I must go into prisons so that I can show prisoners that God has better plans for their lives than the plans they have for their lives. Because I understand their hopelessness, I can offer them hope. I must demonstrate to those behind prison walls God's love for them, just as Jesus showed God's love to me. They need to know Jesus will meet them right where they are.

Anger and bitterness can cause individuals who are incarcerated to place blame everywhere except where it belongs…on themselves. There was a point in time when I began to ask, "Why do I do the things I do, and why do I think the way I think?" I really did not have to look very far to find the answers. I just had to take a good, long look at myself. I kept blaming something or someone else for all my problems. Consequently, I failed to learn the lessons that God wanted me to learn.

I was unable to see that I was the reason I kept going from one messy situation to another. God is not responsible for the decisions we make that cause our lives to crash and burn. Human beings have free will to choose, and we alone are responsible for the messes we make.

As a child, I was not held accountable for my actions. Therefore, I grew up to be an adult who thought nothing I ever did was wrong. I had to learn that accountability, integrity, and responsibility are what would keep me grounded in reality. I had to discover that when I made a mistake, I had to own it and learn from it. I had to be the same person behind closed doors as I am in public.

We live in a world that is continuously changing. Some of those changes are for good, but others lead humanity from one dark place to another. I have been called to help inmates understand how cultural changes can impact their lives and to be aware of the pitfalls.

There will always be those who fight for change and those who will fight against change. There will be those who accept responsibility for their actions, and those who will refuse to be accountable for what they do. I have been called to show others that change can happen, but if you want to change you must:

Accept responsibility for your actions,

Take ownership of your mistakes,

Be accountable for your results,

Trust that God loves you,

Call on the Holy Spirit to guide you,

Let Jesus change you.

And so, these are just a few of the reasons why I do what I do, but make no mistake—I am depending on Jesus every step of the way

CHAPTER 17

WRAPPING UP THE BROKEN PIECES

Although my story is far from over, this seems to be a good place to begin winding down. I look to my future with high expectation for what God is going to do with my life. He has promised in His Word that He is faithful to complete the work He has begun in His children…and He is not through with Ron Zaucha.

It has been painful and challenging for me to go back and relive my heartbreaking life. I am not proud of my past. However, I am so grateful that I finally realized I had to take full responsibility for the terrible choices I made if I was going to change. By God's grace, I have changed, and I am continuing to be transformed. Maturing as a Christian is a never-ending journey, and the more I surrender my life to Jesus, the more I become the man He created me to be…a man with a thankful heart.

I am thankful I made the ultimate life-changing decision to become a follower of Jesus Christ. I daily seek to be Christ-like in every area of my life.

I am thankful I committed my life to following Jesus. The price I paid was total, absolute surrender to His will for my life. The payoff was the gift of eternal life with God.

I am thankful I no longer have unreal expectations of others, especially born-again Christians. Professing to be a believer does not automatically make anyone a perfect human being. Every person on this planet is on a journey, and every journey is different. I have no right to judge another person's journey.

I am thankful I have forgiven those who have hurt me, expecting nothing in return.

I am thankful I have forgiven myself for hurting others.

I am thankful my spiritual rewards in this life have been greater than my earthly losses.

I am thankful Jesus took my self-centeredness and made me other-centered.

I am thankful that each day I know I must die to self.

Ephesians 6:12 teaches, "For we do not wrestle against flesh and blood, but against principalities, against powers, against the rulers of the darkness of this age, against spiritual hosts of wickedness in the heavenly places." I am thankful I have the power to overcome and rise above the enemy of my soul, Satan. He has tried, unsuccessfully, to destroy my faith, my testimony, and my ministry. I am living proof that he is not all-powerful. The power of God's Holy Spirit is available to all who receive Jesus as Savior.

I am thankful God has continued to allow me to do prison ministry, speak in churches, and partner with other ministries.

I am thankful God supplies all my needs. There are times when I wonder how I will pay the bills, but God is always there with me and meets my every need...sometimes at the very last moment.

I am thankful for faithful partners and others who support my ministry. I rely solely on donations to help fund the tracts, Bible studies,

Bible lessons, Bibles, devotionals, and this book—*From Lockdown to Freedom*— to prisoners.

I am thankful for those who give their time and talent to the ministry. I recruit and train volunteers and raise financial support for this self-supporting ministry. I love and appreciate all who are there to serve along with me.

I am thankful I have learned to walk by faith.

I am thankful for His faithfulness to me.

I am thankful God entrusted me with Lighthouse Educational Ministries, Inc. I am even grateful for the frustrations, heartaches, and trials I have endured. They have only caused me to stretch, grow, and mature in Christ. I honestly do not believe this prison ministry would have been birthed had I not gone through them.

I am thankful for the vision God gave me for the ministry. The word "lighthouse" reflects a Christian's call to be the light of the world. The light of God lives within us, and as Christians our bodies are the house, or the temple, of the Holy Spirit. The word "educational" represents the aspect of teaching about Jesus to develop and mature Christians within the Body of Christ.

I am thankful that, by God's grace and faithfulness, over 30,000 souls have been led to faith in Christ through this ministry.

I am thankful for the privilege of being Jesus to inmates through this ministry. As of this writing, it has been for over 24 years, and I have loved every minute of it.

I am thankful for what God is going to do in the future for inmates through Lighthouse Educational Ministries (LEM). I pray Jesus will accomplish more than I can imagine. And if there be any praise for anything I do, I desire that it goes to my Father God and Jesus my Savior.

I am closing the pages of my book with the words of a song entitled *Broken Pieces*. It reflects how God looks at the broken pieces of every person's life. The words to this song touch the core of my own brokenness—perhaps it will affect yours as well.

I am thankful God has taken all of my broken pieces and used them for good.

Broken Pieces[v]

by Chalmer Lumary

I am the light that guides you,

The one you strive to please each day.

Don't worry child today's a new day.

I'll lift you up, and you will hear me say.

For you I died, I took your sins away.

One day you'll kneel before my throne.

So if your life seems to have slipped away,

Just call my name cause you are not alone.

Give these pieces, give your life.

Give your burdens all your pride.

I'll take your heart, and I'll make it new,

make it new for you.

Chorus

I find beauty in your broken pieces.

Come to me oh child of mine.

I find beauty in your broken pieces.

I can see right through, the heart of you.

Right through your heart.

I find beauty. I find beauty.

I find beauty in your broken pieces

Whether you are an inmate who is locked down in prison or someone feeling locked down by the many struggles and destructive issues in your life, I want you to know you are not forgotten. God never sleeps, and he never stops watching; His love for you never changes. Jesus died for you just like He died for me. Jesus is the real deal, and He loves you no matter what you have done. He is waiting for you to come to Him because He finds beauty in your broken pieces and will take you *from lockdown to freedom*.

I want to thank you for taking the time to read my story. Whether you are an inmate, an ex-inmate, a born again Christian or not, I hope my story has been a blessing and an encouragement to you. If you are a Christ follower, please pray that God will provide ways to get *From Lockdown to Freedom* into the hands of prisoners all over the world. Also pray that He will use it to bring healing and to lead many to faith in Jesus…to His glory. And please pray for me and all those who minister to those who are locked behind prison doors.

The following sections are not part of my story. I have included them to provide clarification, teaching, and assistance to prison inmates who are not Christ followers or who are new in their faith. You will also find testimonials of individuals who were directly affected by Lighthouse Educational Ministries, resource information, short summaries about the author and co-author of *From Lockdown to Freedom*.

STEPPING STONES TO FREEDOM^{vi}

The first stepping stone from lockdown to freedom is Jesus Christ. Although there are other stepping stones to freedom, accepting Jesus as your Lord and Savior is the most important step you will ever take. I mean that with all my heart and state it without a shadow of a doubt. It does not matter who you are, where you are, or what you have done. If you take this step, you will experience true freedom of the heart and soul. You will taste life in its fullness as you see God's goodness, mercy, and Grace. You will experience His deep love for you personally and individually. It is the most powerful step available to mankind today, and many have taken it and found freedom beyond imagination.

Imagine for a moment that you are sitting in prison. In fact, you are on death row, and you are sentenced to die. You are guilty, waiting for the final judgment. Some days you think only about your impending death. Other days you tend to put it out of your thoughts. But your mind always comes back to reality. You cannot escape the truth. There you are, in prison on death row, condemned to die. As the time draws closer to your execution, you sit feeling shameful, lost, and doomed. Then at the eleventh hour, something unimaginable happens; something unheard of occurs. A man comes to the prison to die in your place and to face judgment for you. Why? Just because he loves you.

My friend, that man is Jesus Christ, and He died on the cross on a hill called Calvary.[9] He shed His precious blood for you. He did so to pardon you, to set you free from the eternal death row and the judgment of sin. Romans 5:8-9 says in the Bible, "But God demonstrates his own love for us, in that while we were still sinners, Christ died for us. Much more then because we have now been declared righteous by his blood. We will be saved through him from God's wrath." That, my friend, is the depth of God's Grace for us. He loves us so much.

The step to Calvary, the place where Jesus died on a cross, will set you free. "If the Son, therefore, will make you free, you will be free indeed" John 8:36. You take this step simply but sincerely. You must first admit you are a sinner. Romans 3:23 says "All have sinned and come short of the glory of God."[10]

This *all* means just that—ALL. Realizing that we are sinners makes us conscious of our need for a mediator, a Savior. Romans 6:23 says: "For the wages of sin is death, but the free gift of God is eternal life through Jesus Christ our Lord." We must accept that what God's Word says is true and believe on Jesus Christ as our Lord and Savior and ask God to forgive us of our sins and for Jesus to be Lord of our lives. "Everyone who will call upon the name of the Lord will be saved." Romans 10:13

That is the step to the Calvary, the cross where Jesus died, and ultimately the step to freedom, freedom from deep inner misery and suffering in your soul. Many people, although physically free, are in bondage and enslavement and addiction to sin. They are in the prison of sin. Alcohol, drugs, pornography, unbridled lust, greed, and shamelessness consume them and eat them alive. They are shackled and chained

---

9 Calvary is the name of the hill, near Jerusalem in Israel, on which Jesus was crucified.

10 The *glory* of God is the never-ending *greatness* of God. He is the greatest, most powerful, the highest in authority and power. His *glory* is the beauty of perfect love which comes from His perfect character and it is available for all to see and to experience. He is pure, faultless, complete, excellent, incomparable, first, foremost, highest, final.

to sin, to Satan and the world. This is what drugs, sex, rock 'n' roll, pot, booze, pills, and all of Satan's cheap thrills do to one's life. They enslave and imprison. Only at Calvary and through looking to Jesus will you find authentic and genuine freedom.

At Calvary, you will experience the sweet wonders of God's grace and the epitome and fullness of His love. Grace is unmerited favor. It is undeserved. Man does not deserve God's grace and cannot work for it or earn it through works, self-effort, or religion. It is not by works or how many doors you knock on or how many little pamphlets you distribute; it's by grace. We cannot work for it or earn it or buy it. Martin Luther said that "the most damnable and deadly heresy that has ever plagued the mind of man was the idea that somehow he could make himself good enough to deserve to live with an all-Holy God." The step to Calvary, the cross of Jesus, is by grace. Paul says in Eph 2:8-9, "For by grace are you saved through faith and not of yourselves. It is the gift of God, not of works, lest any man should boast." Without God's grace, we would be on the eternal death row...sinners on the way to hell.

God loved us when we did not deserve His love, and because of His deep love, he has provided for us a way to escape sin's punishment. The way is through the death of His Son on the cross of Calvary. He has delivered us from the eternal death row through the stepping stones of Calvary. His grace, His love through His shed blood, give us freedom. In Jesus and only in Him will one find freedom, fulfillment in life, and forgiveness of sin. Don't die on the eternal death row and suffer the never-ending punishment of hell.

Please, please take the step to freedom...the step to Calvary, the cross of Jesus. "Give careful thought to the path of your feet, and be steadfast in all your ways." Proverbs 4:26 Pray and let God minister to your heart and soul through the Lord Jesus Christ. Call upon Him for forgiveness, and look to Him for life! Proverbs 8:35 says, "For those who find me find life and will receive favor from the Lord." In Jesus, you will find favor, fullness, forgiveness, and freedom.

BLUEPRINT FOR PRISON INMATES

A New Life

A. The Stepping Stones

1. Accept Jesus Christ as your Savior.

2. Ask Him to forgive your sins.

3. Ask Him to be the Lord of your life.

4. Ask the Holy Spirit to guide you and help you become like Jesus.

5. Surrender your life and follow him.

6. Read and study God's Word, the Bible.

B. Get a Plan

1. Get a list of transitional halfway houses/Christian homes.

2. Have at least one place to go as soon as you are released.

3. Choose faith, not fear.

4. Let go of pride.

5. Prisoners/inmates: follow the rules.

C. Family and Friends

Dismiss ALL old friends or family members who are a bad influence on you.

Bad influence corrupts good morals. This is what worked for me. After my release, I took the time to call all my old associates. I told each of them the following: "I am a Christian now, and I want no part of our past relationship. Forget my name, my phone number, and forget you know me unless you want to become a Christian like I am. If you want that, by all means call me, but if not, don't contact me again." My weakness was that I struggled with temptation.

Remember that I faced many crossroads in my past, but as I told you in Chapter 14, I received a call from a friend who was basically tempting me to get back into the whole lifestyle I had been set free from. In hindsight, I should never have gone anywhere near the temptation, but I did. I was blessed because at the last minute I chose to walk away. Never forget choices have consequences.

D. Establish New Relationships

1. Find a good Bible-teaching church.

2. Join a Bible study group and a prayer group.

3. Participate in a support group for drug and alcohol addiction.

4. Find an accountability and prayer partner.

Make sure that you connect with the right brothers and sisters within the Body of Christ. I have learned from experience that one must learn the foundations of faith which are why points 1, 2, 3, and 4 are so crucial. I have learned the lesson of trust through the struggles and the trials I endured. The reason I say that is because I learned the hard way that neither churches nor people are perfect. Don't have unreal expectations so that when the trials and disappointments come you will not be disappointed. Keep your eyes on faith in God through Jesus. Remember when adversity comes we must choose to look at it as either a burden or a bridge. If you allow it to become a burden, you will most likely give up, but if you look at it as a bridge you will walk over the bridge to the other side of adversity… to freedom.

E. Employment

   1. Look for job information in the newspapers and on the internet.

   2. Register at the unemployment office.

   3. Network among friends and in your church or other organizations.

   4. Embrace new skills—get your GED if you didn't finish high school.

   5. Enroll in college or a trade school.

   6. Don't give up; keep trying.

After I got out of prison, I attended seminary school at Vision International University. I received my B.A. in Theology with an emphasis on Chaplaincy Studies and spent ten years taking Bible Study courses through Calvary Chapel of Costa Mesa. I also became an ordained, licensed minister.

   7. Don't let your pride stop you from asking for help.

Don't set your sights too high with false expectations. I would tell myself, "Say yes to crappy jobs and build on that not-so-glamorous job. It may have great possibilities in the future." Recall in Chapter 12 when my shoveling horse manure days turned into a management position? Most people have to start at the bottom and work their way up in any place of business. Besides, it's good for your soul and ego. Believe that you will improve and succeed as time goes on. Be a good employee, work hard, be faithful, and be patient with yourself, others, and yes, even God who has a plan that you might not see right away. Don't ever stop looking forward.

F. Keep a journal/prayer partner notebook

This may be difficult at first, but it helps to keep track of your thoughts and your failures and your successes. This can be a vehicle that will help you look back and see that life was not all bad all the time…at least not as bad as you thought it was.

G. Facts about those who make it after they get out of jail or prison

1. Parolees have others in their lives to help.

2. They found a church, which gave them support.

3. The support the church gave was both spiritual and financial.

4. The help provided by the church was freely given and for as long as needed.

5. Each person employed lots of self-discipline in turning himself/herself around.

6. Each parolee exerted a lot of patience.

7. It was not easy.

H. Facts about those who don't make it after they get out of jail/prison

1. Parolees failed to avoid situations which would lead them into trouble.

2. They had no job or trade.

3. They were under the influence of drugs or alcohol.

4. They had no one to talk to.

5. They had no friends or family, no community support or encouragement.

Don't let your circumstances determine your final outcome. You have the power to make different choices for your life. Don't by the lie that life can never be better.

I. Stinking thinking

   1. I must have a job at the top.

      a. Be willing to start at the bottom and work to the top.

      b. Follow orders to demonstrate a willingness to learn.

   2. I deserve the best.

      a. Learn to think before buying anything.

      b. Find someone to teach how to live on a budget.

      c. Be disciplined and learn to live within a budget.

   3. Nobody's going to tell me what to do.

      a. Learn to accept advice and instructions.

      b. Be self-discipline as taught within the regimented prison atmosphere.

      c. Go the extra mile.

ROMAN ROAD TO SALVATION

Finding the way to Christ is simple, and the Roman Road is a great example that will lead you to Him. It walks you through the scriptures that the Apostle Paul wrote to the Roman church. It will help you understand everyone's sinful condition, and it will show you how the wrong in your life can be made right through the Savior, Jesus Christ.

The problem is sin

Admitting that you are a sinner is the first step on the Roman Road. When Adam and Eve disobeyed God in the Garden of Eden, they committed the first sin. Since that time every human has been born with the problem of having a sin nature.

Romans 3:10 As it is written, there is no one righteous, not even one.
Romans 3:23 For all have sinned, and come short of the glory of God.
Romans 5:12 For just as sin entered into the world by one man, and death through sin and in this way death came to all people because all sinned.

The bad news is there is a price to pay

Because of sin, there is a wage, or a payment, for sin. Death is what we deserve because we owe a debt for our sin. The place that God has prepared for sinners is called Hell. God owes us nothing, but He gives us unearned kindness.

Romans 6:23a For the wages of sin is death, but the gift of God is eternal life in Christ Jesus our Lord.

The good news is a free gift

God loves us so much that He offers the gift of His Son, Jesus who paid our sin debt for us. When we believe that Jesus died for us to pay our debt, our destination changes from Hell to Heaven; we receive eternal life with God.

Romans 6:23b But the gift of God is eternal life through Jesus Christ our Lord
Romans 5:8 But God demonstrates his own love for us, in this: While we were still sinners, Christ died for us.
Romans 10:13 For everyone who calls upon the name of the Lord shall be saved.

You have a choice to make

You do not need to do anything because Jesus did everything for you.
God wants to hear from you.
He wants to hear you confess that you are a sinner.
He wants to hear that you believe Jesus died on the cross for you.
He wants to hear you acknowledge that you are forgiven of your sins.
He wants to hear you ask Jesus to come into your life and to be the Lord of your life.

He wants to hear you invite the Holy Spirit into your life.

Romans 10:9-10 If you declare with your mouth, "Jesus is Lord," and believe in your heart that God raised him from the dead, you will be saved. For it is with your heart that you believe and become justified (made right before God), and it is with your mouth that you profess your faith and are saved.

Say the salvation prayer

Father, I know that I have broken your laws and my sins have separated me from you. I am truly sorry, and now I want to turn away from my past sinful life toward you. Please forgive me, and help me avoid sinning again. I believe that your son Jesus Christ died for my sins, was resurrected from the dead, is alive, and hears my prayer. I invite you, Jesus, to become the Lord of my life, to rule and reign in my heart from this day forward. Please send your Holy Spirit to help me obey You and to do Your will for the rest of my life. In Jesus' name, I pray, Amen.

Be baptized

Repent, and let every one of you be baptized in the name of Jesus Christ for the remission of sins and you shall receive the gift of the Holy Spirit. Acts 2:38

Be a witness for Jesus

Jesus told his disciples just before he ascended into Heaven to go into all the world and preach the good news to all creation. Acts1:8

The Spirit of the Sovereign Lord is upon me, for the Lord has anointed me to bring good news to the poor. He has sent me to comfort the brokenhearted and to proclaim that captives will be released and prisoners will be freed. Isaiah 61:1

TESTIMONIALS

Michael

I am 32 years old. My mom and dad are bikers, and I was introduced to drugs and beer at the age of 10. By the time I was 13, I was drinking day and night, using coke, smoking pot, and stealing everything in sight. By the time I turned 14, I was the cool kid in the Cad rolling along with the gold around my neck and a 357 magnum at my side.

One night I was lying on my bed in Chino Prison, and a guy said there was a meeting going on, kind of like a Bible Study. At first, the thought of this just made me mad. The next week the same guy asked me to join him. I thought what the heck, it will get me out of my little cell. Little did I know this one hour would change my life.

When I walked in, I met this guy who said his name was Ron Zaucha. He spoke of a new way of life. But not until he gave his testimony did I really begin to listen. By the time he was done, it was like someone reached out and lit a match to the pilot light in my heart. It gave me a flicker of hope. When we were done sharing a part of our lives, we prayed. After my fourth time going to his class, my mind began to clear. And the more I read my Bible, the more I saw that this was not the life the Lord had in store for me.

Our Father says to follow Him, and He will not lead us down the wrong path. He says He will send us angels to show us the right way. I do believe Ron Zaucha is an angel. The Lord is working through him to show us a better way of life while here on earth.

Cynthia

Lighthouse Ministries gave me the strength to go on while I was in prison. After my release, Lighthouse was there for me with a job, resources, and all the help that I needed to get on my feet and care for my nine children. Because of Lighthouse Ministries, I have a future.

Paul

Truly, Lighthouse has the heart for the lost. The lost know this and respond. Lighthouse is a breath of fresh air from above, teaching and leading through discipleship—just as our Lord commanded! With Lighthouse, the mission is realized—to wean from milk to meat.

Brett

I've been in and out of prison for the last ten years. I want to learn how to apply God's wisdom to my life because I am addicted to shooting speed, and the only way I'm ever going to stop is to apply Jesus' Word to my life and ask Him for the strength to stop. It's the sin of doing drugs that always leads me back to places like this. Ron's classes have opened my eyes.

Shelia

I am so blessed to have the opportunity to be taught the Word by your ministry. Enclosed is a small donation.

John

I am 42 years old and I'm tired of the life drugs have given me. I've tried so many times to do things right, but it always comes out wrong. I have never before been involved in a program, and I truly feel that I need to seek guidance in areas of my life like parenting, anger management, and drug abuse. I have three children, and I'm doing this for the benefit of my kids and ultimately for myself.

Dane

I personally have learned from your teaching that Jesus is so very real! And the insight that you were able to display to us about who Jesus really was, and still is, is very remarkable in my heart.

Vincent

As a Christian, there are basic foundational areas in my life that have been lacking spiritual growth. The growth in these areas that I could not have received any other way except through your ministry is extremely vital to my success and maturity as a child of God. As I grow in this relationship, I believe the years lost to the locusts of the world will be restored unto me. I also believe I will never have to return to environments such as this.

Ricky

Hearing Ron's testimony and past experience with prison give me hope to face the challenges that he has overcome through his faith in Jesus Christ. His ministry is a breath of life. He gets involved with us personally, and his approach is very effective.

Janet

I'm writing this letter to you to let you know how much I appreciate you and your ministry team. I have included a small donation.

ABOUT THE AUTHOR

Ron Zaucha,

Executive Director/Founder
Lighthouse Educational Ministries Inc.
(Lighthouseedministries.org)

Having been incarcerated and paroled, Ron Zaucha understands the difficulty of surviving behind prison walls. He also can relate to the struggle of becoming self-reliant after being released from prison. After an incredibly personal experience with Jesus while in prison, his heart's desire was to learn who Jesus is, to get to know Him, and do His will. Ron's love for Jesus grew into a passion for helping prisoners and for prison ministry.

Three years after being released from prison in 1990, Ron got involved in Steinkamp Prison Ministries. Eventually, he became Administrator and Director of the nationwide Bible study correspondence course for prisoners.

Ron's friend and mentor, Mel Novak, encouraged Ron to start his own prison ministry. In 2001, Ron Founded Lighthouse Educational Ministries Inc.(LEM), a nonprofit, self-supporting ministry. LEM has ministered in the California State Penitentiary system for women for over 20 years and the Chuckwalla Valley State Prison for more than 7 years. Ron has ministered in the Chino Men's Prison, California Youth

Authority, Orange County Jails, L.A. County Jails, the Fred Jordan Mission, and Mel Novak's skid row ministry in Los Angeles, California.

Ron graduated from seminary school at Vision International University in 2001. He received his B.A. in Theology with an emphasis on Chaplaincy Studies to become a State Prison Chaplain. He also spent ten years taking Bible Study courses through Calvary Chapel of Costa Mesa and is an ordained, licensed Minister of the Gospel of Jesus Christ.

During his time with Chaplain Wally Nelson, Ron had the pleasure of meeting and working with Chaplain Ray and Bill Glass Prison Ministries based in Dallas, Texas. He personally worked with Chuck Colson and his Prison Fellowship Ministry based out of Washington, D.C. and worked on projects with California Rehabilitation Center in Norco, California and Chuckawalla Valley State Prison in Blythe, California and Kairos Prison Ministry. He took Celebrate Recovery, which is a 12-step biblically-based program designed to help those struggling with "hurts, habits, and hang-ups", into prisons with men from Saddleback Church in Lake Forest, California.

Ron served as Associate Pastor at Loveland Church in Fontana, California and has appeared on The Christian Broadcasting Network program, *The 700 Club*, and The Trinity Broadcasting Network, TBN. Currently, he is on the pastoral teaching staff of Orange County Singles for Christ Church, continues to manage LEM and work with other ministries when time allows.

ABOUT THE CO-AUTHOR

Nola Katherine
Author, I Can Begin Again
nolakatherinetrewin.com

Throughout her adult life, Nola Katherine has led Bible studies, prayer groups and retreats on forgiveness. She has also spoken to small groups and churches. Nola Katherine has been a repeated guest of Dr. Gene Getz on his weekly program, Renewal Radio, and was interviewed on the American Family Radio program, Today's Issues. She is the Author of *I Can Begin Again*, Inside the Mind of an Adult Who was Abused as a Child and is now co-authoring and ghostwriting for other authors.

As important as these experiences are, she feels her most purposeful moments are one-on-one, sometimes unexpected, encounters with those who are suffering. She is especially drawn to those who endure the devastating effects of child abuse. For this reason, she chose to overcome her fears, to be vulnerable, and tell her own, personal story of sexual abuse. It is her desire for others to experience the freedom she now has from the horrific power her abusers had over her for forty years. She believes that no one should ever have to carry their abuser's anger, guilt, and shame...especially for so long.

Nola Katherine lives in the Dallas area with Jake, her soulmate of 50 years. Her three children, their spouses, and her five grandchildren bring her immeasurable joy and keep her young. She is thankful to God, Jesus, and the Holy Spirit for their presence in her life.

At the age of 75, she continues to write for herself and others and, enjoys a full active life.

SOURCE REFERENCES

i   Sin City - The movie *Casino* depicts the Las Vegas scene. It is a 1995 crime drama based on the true story of Frank Rosenthal who ran three casinos in Las Vegas for the Chicago Outfit from the 1970s until the early 1980s.

ii   Conduct Disorder (CD) is a serious behavioral and emotional disorder that can occur in children and teens. A child with this disorder may display a pattern of disruptive and violent behavior and have problems following rules. Behavior is considered to be a Conduct Disorder when it is long-lasting and when it violates the rights of others, goes against accepted norms of behavior and disrupts the child's or family's everyday life. In general, symptoms of conduct disorder fall into four general categories: Aggressive behavior, destructive behavior, deceitful behavior, and violation of rules. In addition, many children with CD are irritable, have low self-esteem, and tend to throw frequent temper tantrums. Some may abuse drugs and alcohol. Children with CD often are unable to appreciate how their behavior can hurt others and generally have little guilt or remorse about hurting others.

https://www.webmd.com/mental-health/mental-health-conduct-disorder#1

iii   I Can Begin Again, Inside the Mind of an Adult Who was Abused as a Child, Nola Katherine Trewin.com, Amazon.com, Barnes & Noble.

iv   Google Cocaine Cowboy for information about the drug scene in Florida.

v   Broken Pieces by Chalmer Lumary. CD of this song is available through Lighthouseedministries.org for a donation.

vi   Stepping Stone to Freedom by Mickey Park, Inmate Missionary.

Information about Poland, the Chicago mafia, prohibition, culture trends from the 1950s through the 1990s, including racial tensions, can be found on the Internet.

Bible scripture references come from the New International Version (NIV) unless otherwise indicated.